Dance Me a Story

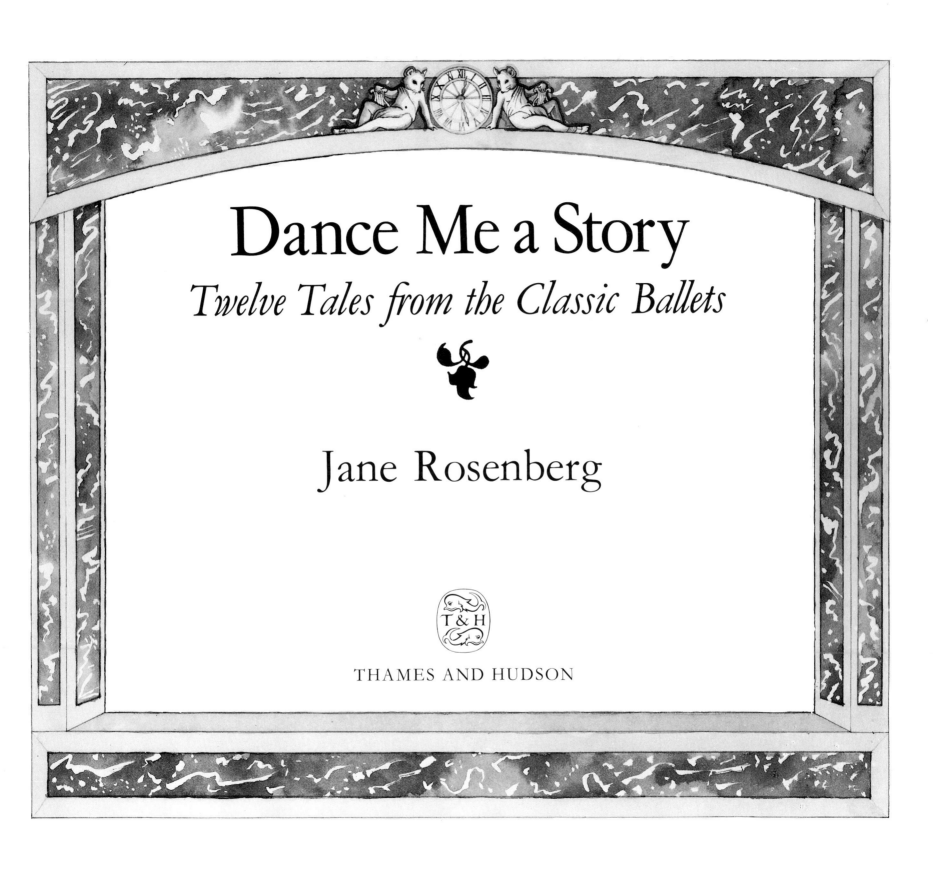

Dance Me a Story

Twelve Tales from the Classic Ballets

Jane Rosenberg

THAMES AND HUDSON

For Lily and Abner Rosenberg

Contents

Introduction

A child's first introduction to the ballet is most often with a familiar and well-loved story such as *The Nutcracker*. Parents hope that the splendor and pageantry of the spectacle will provide a memorable experience, even if the dancing is not fully appreciated. They realize, however, that the pantomime and story line may be confusing, and so, when they arrive at the theater, they are likely to read through the brief synopsis in the program in order to refresh their memories before trying to acquaint their children with the plot and characters.

These hasty last-minute efforts, however, often have little effect. The great full-length ballets of the world are complex fairy tales which are not easily encapsulated in a synopsis and swallowed in a single gulp, especially by a child. The scenery, costumes, music, and dancing will always exert their charm, but failure to understand the story as it unfolds, or to notice certain small but telling details, will remain an obstacle to full enjoyment.

Anyone looking for a sensitive and comprehensive introduction to these ballets will surely welcome *Dance Me a Story*. It brings to life twelve of the world's best-loved full-length ballets, works that have cast an enduring spell over generations of spectators of all ages. The beautiful illustrations, based on actual productions and rich in fanciful detail, together with an evocative, eminently readable text, vividly re-create each ballet. This, then, is more than an inspiring introduction to a wonderful new world: for many it will be an enlightening and entertaining portrayal of familiar stories.

The text clarifies many aspects of the ballets that are mysterious and potentially confusing: Who are the Wilis? Why is Petrouchka unhappy? Why does Swanilda shake the wheat? What is Dr. Coppélius doing to Franz and Swanilda in Act II? Much of the difficulty in understanding the action in ballet lies in the traditional use of pantomime to convey crucial elements of the plot. Since the conventions of pantomime are often unfamiliar to the average ballet-goer, Jane Rosenberg has cleverly forearmed the reader by interspersing her narrative with timely bits of dialogue which shed light on what the pantomime was intended to express. She has also included descriptions of the music, which help to create not only the atmosphere of the ballet but also the impression of sitting in a theater listening to the music as the performance takes place.

The illustrations capture the atmosphere and scenery of each ballet. These eye-catching paintings, set within a proscenium arch, range from bright and cheerful to dark and foreboding. No photograph could bring out the colors and wealth of detail that these watercolors do. They encourage the reader to create his or her own fantasies, while at the same time they set the scene of each ballet: the quaint, picturesque village of *Coppélia*, the mysterious Scottish moors and farmhouse of *La Sylphide*, the gaiety of the carnival scenes in *Petrouchka*. There is great variety in the scenes depicted, and each painting has a beauty all its own.

Unlike a ballet in live performance, when the myriad details and the action flash by, defying the quickest eye, here the text and the pictures stand still, allowing time for reverie and review. Later, when one enters the reality of the theater, it will be with a keener eye and clearer understanding, and the result, quite simply, will be greater appreciation and pleasure.

Between the covers of this book lies a fairy-tale world which is neither too naive for adults nor too sophisticated for the youngest child, and everyone is sure to be touched by the enchanted and enchanting world it re-creates.

Merrill Ashley

Cinderella

Act I

Cinderella, dressed in rags and covered with soot, kneels by the fire polishing silver. Her two stepsisters—the ugliest women in the kingdom—are seated nearby embroidering a scarf to wear to the royal ball. Jealous of Cinderella's youth and beauty, the ugly sisters have made her a servant in her own home. Even Cinderella's father cannot protect her from his stepdaughters, so envious are they.

The stepsisters are a silly-looking pair in their little black boots and ruffled caps as they squabble over who will wear the scarf to the ball.

"It's mine!" screeches the elder sister, who stands tall and thin.

"It's not!" squeaks the younger, who is short and squat.

"I'm suffocating!" cries the former, having accidentally wound the scarf around her throat.

"Serves you right!" chimes the latter, and she pulls at the scarf till it rips in two.

Their stepfather finally convinces them to patch up their quarrel. After exchanging reluctant kisses, the old maids dance together, each with her own piece of scarf. Linking arms, up the stairs they go, chattering and bickering, to prepare for the ball. Their henpecked stepfather follows meekly behind.

Cinderella looks after them wistfully, for she too longs to go to the ball. As she sweeps the floor, she dreams of happy days past. In spite of her rags, she is much prettier than any other woman in the kingdom.

Sadly, Cinderella lights a candle and places it on the mantel in front of her mother's portrait. Her father finds her grieving before the painting, and he feels

The old maids dance together, each with her own piece of scarf.

8

ashamed. He loves his daughter and knows it's partly his fault that she suffers. The stepsisters soon return to discover father and daughter embracing.

"None of that!" they shriek, jealously pulling the two apart.

Suddenly an eerie melody overpowers their voices and rushes like a chill wind through the house. The two stepsisters clutch each other in fear. A black-cloaked beggarwoman comes through the kitchen door, a gnarled hand extended, her body stooped with age. The ugly sisters are disgusted and order her away, but Cinderella, unafraid of the mysterious hag, feels only pity and offers her a loaf of bread. The elder stepsister wags a pointed finger and scolds Cinderella for her wasteful ways, but her jaw is magically frozen in midsentence, forcing her into silence. The old beggarwoman takes Cinderella's lovely, smiling face in her hand.

"I know a kindhearted soul when I meet one. Thank you for your generosity," she says, and goes on her way.

The ugly stepsisters only recover from their shock with the arrival of the haberdasher and his assistants, who have come to prepare them for the ball. The sisters bask in the attention of hatmakers, jewelers, shoemakers, and maids, believing their beauty deserves the best. When the tall one removes her cap to try on a bonnet, she reveals a nearly bald head and looks even sillier than before.

Corsets are laced tighter and tighter to hold in bulging flesh, enormous hands are squeezed into dainty gloves, and wrinkled necks are adorned with pearls and gems. The ridiculous effect is completed with the addition of cone-shaped wigs. The tall sister wears a black wig, perched on her head like a bird's nest, while the short sister, in strawberry blond, has a head like a carrot.

The dancing master now arrives with his violinists to teach the old maids the gavotte, a fast-paced dance that was the current fashion at court. Each sister takes one of the instructor's hands, and although the elder seems competent enough, the younger moves her feet clumsily, stepping on everyone's toes. The ugly sisters compete for the dancing master's favor, pulling him this way and that, but eventually wind up in each other's arms instead.

Time is growing short, and a coach arrives to take the sisters and their stepfather to the ball. Cinderella begs her father to let her go too, but he dare not disobey his stepdaughters. Embarrassed, he hurries after them, leaving poor Cinderella to her tears and her solitude. She looks sadly at her mother's portrait, and then, remembering the steps taught by the dancing master, tries them herself. Pretending her broom is a handsome prince, she ties a scarf around the stick and waltzes with it as her partner.

"I do wish I could go. What fun it would be to dance at the prince's palace!"

A sudden draft makes a door bang. The kitchen darkens inexplicably, and once again the eerie music invades the room. The black-cloaked hag has returned.

"Are you still hungry?" asks Cinderella.

"No, child," she answers and throws off her cape. Cinderella is astonished to discover she is not a wrinkled old beggar but a beautiful woman.

"I am your fairy godmother, and I make wishes come true. Because of your kindness you shall go to the ball. But first we must visit my helpers, the Fairies of the Four Seasons."

With a wave of her wand, the walls of the room fly away and Cinderella finds herself transported to a cool glade by a tumbling waterfall. There, flanked by shepherds, is the Spring Fairy, dressed in grass green. Like a mischievous faun romping through the forest, she dances.

"On to summer," says the fairy godmother, and the banks of a river magically appear. The Summer Fairy, her yellow curls decked with a crown of flowers, bows to Cinderella and dances to a languid melody.

The scene changes again, and deep in the woods the Autumn Fairy, in her orange tutu and leaf headdress, tosses leaves into the wind.

Pretending her broom is a handsome prince, Cinderella ties a scarf around the stick and waltzes with it as her partner.

Cinderella ACT II

Finally they travel to a white landscape, where the castle of the Winter Fairy rises on a distant glacier. Her arms glitter with icicle pendants, and diamonds adorn her hair. She dances elegantly, moving her arms as if scooping up snow from the earth.

The Fairies of the Four Seasons, led by the fairy godmother, dance with warmth in their hearts for Cinderella; but the gay music turns threatening, a signal for the fairy godmother to give her warning.

"Though you will go to the ball as richly dressed as any princess, you must return home by midnight or you will find yourself standing before the court in your poor rags."

A bell chimes twelve to remind Cinderella of the fateful hour.

Cinderella nods. "I understand, and I thank you with all my heart."

"Good! Now find me a pumpkin and some mice and we'll get ready," says the fairy godmother.

While Cinderella leaves to gather the necessary items, the fairy godmother summons her attendants, a constellation of twinkling stars, who dance in crossing patterns to a wondrous waltz.

Cinderella returns with the pumpkin, and as the Fairies of the Four Seasons join the dance, the fairy godmother transports them to the bottom of the winding road that leads to the prince's palace. The skies have cleared, and with a last wave of the magic wand, the pumpkin turns into a golden coach, the mice grow into tall footmen with velvet coats, and, best of all, Cinderella's dirt and rags fall away to reveal a beautiful gown. She climbs into her elegant carriage, and the footmen hurry her off to the palace and the ball.

Act II

When the two ugly sisters enter the grand ballroom on their stepfather's arm, the party is in full swing. The court jester is rolling down the marble staircase, cavorting for the guests, and the courtiers are dancing to a spirited march. With the assurance of a vain beauty, the elder sister glides down the steep staircase, coyly waving her large fan of ostrich feathers. The younger sister, in a giant hoop skirt that exposes her shapeless ankles, lingers nervously at the entrance.

The glitter of the chandeliers and the glamour of the crowd frighten her. Both sisters wear huge crowns of ostrich feathers atop their wigs, and their enormous heads appear too large for their bodies.

The elder sister pushes the younger forward.

"Come on now, don't be stupid. Look at all these handsome men."

"But it's all so intimidating," the fat little sister frets, until she is asked to dance by a tall, good-looking captain.

A pompous little man dressed like Napoleon, complete with hand in waistcoat, bows to the elder sister. She's flattered at first but then realizes how short he is. Sizing up the situation, she grabs her sister's tall partner, exchanging him for the stunted Napoleon.

The younger sister wants to show off what she has learned from the dancing master. She begins confidently enough, but soon loses step. Determined to outdo her, the elder sister tries a Spanish fandango and falls over on her ankle. Unabashed, she pulls up her slipping garters and balances on one foot. She is about to topple over when the handsome captain tries to help her. Unfortunately, as she reaches for his hand, he moves, and she stumbles forward into the arms of the laughing jester.

A trumpet sounds and everyone's attention turns to the grand staircase. Prince Charming, dressed in royal blue, his coat studded with diamonds, stands regally at the top of the stairs. The ugly stepsisters grovel at his feet, but he barely notices them as he graciously encourages his guests to dance.

The festivities are interrupted once more as a magical melody takes the court by surprise. Cinderella appears at the top of the stairs, accompanied by the Fairies of the Four Seasons and the constellation of stars.

Prince Charming, enchanted by Cinderella's beauty, climbs the steps to greet her. She takes his hand and descends the staircase with an uncommon grace. The courtiers form a circle around the couple, and as Cinderella dances demurely, Prince Charming leaps with abandon, delighted to have this mysterious princess as his partner. The Fairies of the Four Seasons are invited to dance by the prince's courtiers, and, accompanied by the twinkling stars, they light up the ballroom to the sounds of an exuberant waltz.

Only the ugly stepsisters are unimpressed by the spectacle and the unknown princess.

"She's not bad looking, but why in the world would he choose her over us?" they wonder.

No one has ever seen the prince so happy. Clapping his hands, he calls for his page to present Cinderella with a gift. The page marches in bearing a silver tray with three oranges, the rarest fruit in the kingdom. Cinderella accepts the tribute, yet even in her glory she notices that her two stepsisters feel jealous and neglected. She begs them each to accept an orange, and they do so greedily, fighting and squawking over who deserves the biggest. When the entire court leaves for a stroll in the gardens, the two old maids are still juggling the fruit. Finally they link arms and, heads bobbing, gallop off like a pair of ancient racehorses.

Prince Charming returns alone from the garden to the quiet ballroom.

"Where is Cinderella?" he wonders. "Could she have vanished as mysteriously as she arrived?"

Cinderella emerges from the garden and gazes at her handsome prince with love.

He kisses her hand and, to a slow, tender melody of harp and strings, he lifts her in his arms. As their dance comes to an end, a flute plays serenely, and Cinderella circles her prince and steps into his waiting arms.

Now the twinkling stars and the Fairies of the Four Seasons enter the ballroom and dance to an intoxicating waltz. Arm in arm, Prince Charming and Cinderella turn down an aisle formed by the dancers.

Lost in the music, Cinderella is happier at this moment than ever before in her life. It comes as a terrible shock when the castle bell begins to chime twelve.

"Oh no! I must leave immediately!" she cries.

"But I've only just found you. Wait!" pleads the prince, still holding her arm.

Cinderella tries desperately to leave the ballroom, but the prince does everything he can to restrain her. Running this way and that into groups of partygoers, she hides her face, fearing that her shabby, threadbare clothes will return as quickly as they disappeared. Finally she breaks free from the crowd and, as her ball gown turns to rags, flees up the stairs, leaving behind one of her jeweled slippers.

Confused and despairing, the prince retrieves the slipper, all that is left of his mysterious love.

Cinderella ACT III

Act III

It is a few minutes past midnight, and Cinderella, in her tattered dress, is racing home. The ball has ended and groups of partygoers are close behind. Escorted by two suitors, the ugly stepsisters gallop home, still fighting over the biggest orange.

Accompanied by his jester, the prince begins his quest to find the owner of the jeweled slipper.

*   *   *

Cinderella dozes by the fire, a contented smile on her lips. As she stirs, she realizes she is by her own hearth, no longer in the arms of Prince Charming.

"It must have been a dream," she sighs. "But what a lovely dream it was!"

Feeling something hard in her apron pocket, she reaches in and pulls out a jeweled slipper.

"So, it was real! The ball . . . the palace . . . the prince."

When her stepsisters enter the house, Cinderella quickly hides the slipper again in her pocket.

"Help us with our dresses, Cinderella," they scold. "Can't you see we've had a long night?" She comes to their aid, and they collapse in two chairs in their bloomers and petticoats.

"Please tell me about the ball," Cinderella begs.

"Well," says the elder, "the prince presented us, the most beautiful women at court, with these oranges. And then I danced with a handsome captain the whole evening. Oh, I'm in love!"

"In love!" shrieks the younger. "Why, you stole him from me. He's mine, you hussy!"

Punching and struggling in their underwear, they barely hear their stepfather announce the arrival of the prince.

"Here? Now? What does he want?" they scream. "Our dresses, quick, button them up!"

"He's coming to look for the owner of a jeweled slipper. They say he will marry the girl that it fits," answers their stepfather.

The prince enters and the ugly sisters curtsy. The eldest, who hasn't fastened her buttons, is in such rapture when he kisses her hand that her dress falls down.

"Would you ladies do me the honor of trying this slipper?" the prince asks.

He hands the slipper to his jester, who places a footstool before the younger stepsister. She pushes and shoves, tugs and pulls, finally pounding the jester on his back in a futile effort to get her fat foot into the dainty slipper.

Now it's the elder's turn, and she nearly splinters the stool when she places her heavy foot on it. Her foot gets stuck in the shoe, and when Cinderella bends over to help, the second slipper falls from her apron pocket.

"The matching slipper!" exclaims the prince. Holding Cinderella's face in his hands, he gazes deep into her eyes. "You do look very much like her," he marvels. "Here, try it on, please."

"Impossible!" shriek the old maids.

Cinderella puts the jeweled slippers on her feet without the slightest effort. The prince is not surprised, for he has recognized her grace and beauty, even through her rags.

"I've found you at last and I'll never let you go again. Please say you'll be my bride."

"Cinderella, we had no idea," her awed stepsisters stammer, bowing before her.

Cinderella harbors no ill will. She pities her stepsisters and helps them to their feet.

The fairy godmother magically appears before Cinderella and Prince Charming. She waves her wand and transports them to an enchanted garden where Spring, Summer, Autumn, and Winter dance. Cinderella, dressed once again like a princess, is more radiant than ever. To gentle music, the prince lifts her high in the air, carrying her away to the palace and a life to be lived happily ever after.

— the curtain falls —

Coppélia

Act I

Set among the brightly painted wooden houses of a charming old village square is a dark, stone workshop where mysterious Dr. Coppélius and his shy daughter, Coppélia, live. Today, the grouchy old doctor, in his ill-fitting jacket and wrinkled trousers, is sitting on the bench in front of his workshop. He glances up at the second-story window where Coppélia, the joy of his life, sits reading a book. Blowing her a kiss, he hobbles into the house, closing the door behind him.

Across the square a door opens and out skips the raven-haired Swanilda. She gazes with curiosity at Coppélius's window and waves at his beautiful daughter. Coppélia neither smiles nor waves back. With a low, ceremonious bow, Swanilda invites Coppélia to come down into the square, but the frozen-faced girl doesn't respond. Swanilda shrugs and, unable to repress her tremendous energy and love of life, she dances.

Upon finishing her dance, she catches sight of Franz, her fiancé, making his way toward the square. She quickly hides inside her house and peeks out of the window to see if Franz is up to something with Coppélia, as she suspects.

A comical little tune accompanies the handsome—and conceited—young man. When Franz discovers that Swanilda has stopped dancing and gone inside, he glances at the old doctor's house.

"I'll see if Coppélia wants to come down and dance instead. She's very beautiful—maybe even more beautiful than my Swanilda."

Coppélia ACT I

He blows Coppélia a kiss, but she remains engrossed in her book. Too vain to think he is unwanted, Franz prepares to try again, but he sees the old doctor come to the window, and he quickly hides.

Coppélius smoothes his daughter's ruffled dress and pats her lovingly on the head.

"So Franz sends you kisses, does he? Well, why don't you send him some in return, my doll?"

Obediently, Coppélia stands up and edges closer to the open window. Franz sees her and creeps out of hiding. She blows him two kisses and returns to her seat.

"Success!" he cheers. "She likes me. I'll just ask her to come down and do the same thing cheek to cheek." He smoothes his hair into place, straightens his shirt collar, and shines his boots.

"Lovely lady, won't you join me in the warm afternoon sun?"

Swanilda, watching from her window, hasn't missed a moment of this treacherous performance.

"Why, that two-timer! I'll put a stop to this."

The shrewd Swanilda doesn't want Franz to know she has been spying on him, so she grabs a butterfly net and runs daintily into the square. She catches a butterfly and dances in circles around Franz, waving her prize. Franz takes the butterfly from her and, like a victorious soldier, pins it proudly to his chest.

"You brute! You animal! How could you hurt such a tiny creature?" she storms.

Dumbfounded by her rage, Franz demands, "What did I do that was so terrible?"

"I'll tell you, you double-crossing scoundrel! You deceived me with her," Swanilda shouts, revealing the true cause of her anger. "First you blow kisses at Coppélia, then you ask her to dance with you. I shall never trust you again as long as I live."

"Sweetheart, you can't mean that. You know I love you more than anyone. Now kiss and make up."

"Never!" she swears, pushing him away.

The argument is interrupted as a crowd of their friends—the girls wearing headdresses of ribbons and flowers, the boys in red boots and handsome embroidered waistcoats—dance into the square. The young people want Franz and Swanilda to join them in a mazurka, a lively Polish folk dance.

"Come on, Swanilda. The day is so beautiful—why should we spend it quarreling? Let's dance with our friends."

"Ask someone else. With your charm, you snake, you'll have no trouble."

To Swanilda's dismay, Franz takes her at her word and offers his hand to a waiting girl. In a moment, he has forgotten his fiancée and is swept away by the vigorous, intoxicating music.

The dancing couples click their heels and spin round and round, moving forward and then back again in unison. When the town's mayor enters the square, everyone stops to greet him.

"I have an announcement to make which will be of interest to all you young people," the mayor explains. "Tomorrow we shall hold a festival in honor of our new town bell. Because it's such an important occasion, his lordship will award a handsome dowry to any girls who get married on this day. What do you say to that, Swanilda?"

"She won't answer you, sir. She's angry with me," says Franz. "Perhaps you can convince her that my love is true."

Swanilda describes Franz's infatuation with Coppélia. The mayor takes Swanilda's part and tells Franz that he does seem to have been untrustworthy.

"That's not so. I love Swanilda from the bottom of my heart."

"And a shallow heart it is, you traitor!" replies Swanilda.

"Now, children, stop quarreling and calm down. I know how we can resolve the problem. Swanilda, take this stalk of wheat and shake it. If you hear it rattle, then you can rest assured that Franz loves you."

Smiling shyly, Swanilda inches toward her fiancé. Franz tenderly places his arms around her as she holds the wheat to her ear. She shakes the wheat but hears nothing, and as she tries again, Franz supports her in deep arabesques, then lifts her up to his shoulder. Again the wheat is silent. Swanilda is about to despair of ever hearing the wheat's answer, when Franz kisses her hand reassuringly and sweeps her into a low dive, her head very near the ground, where she shakes the wheat one last time. Neither Swanilda nor Franz can hear it rattle, and Swanilda is in tears. She throws the wheat at his feet and runs from the square as Franz follows, hoping to console her.

Franz leans the ladder against Coppélia's window. He begins to climb.

Their friends, accustomed to their frequent quarrels, decide to dance, knowing full well that Swanilda and Franz will join them before long.

Just as expected, Swanilda skips into the square with Franz close behind. She dances as if she hasn't a care in the world, while Franz leaps boldly around the square, trying to impress her with his flamboyant acrobatics. Swanilda pretends not to notice and dances enticingly, hoping to win him back. But just when Swanilda thinks she has reconquered his straying heart, a gypsy girl asks Franz to be her partner in a Hungarian czardash. He soon forgets his sweetheart, and only when the gypsy leaves with another beau does Franz return to Swanilda. He is amazed to find her angry again.

"It's no use trying to please her when she's in this mood," he declares to his friends. "I give up. Let's have some fun at the tavern, where there won't be any women to bother us."

While the boys go off arm in arm, the girls enter Swanilda's house, and dusk settles on the little village square.

The street lights come on one by one, and, as stars appear in the night sky, Dr. Coppélius shuffles out of his house. Busy locking his front door, he fails to notice Franz and his companions returning from the tavern. The boys like to put on a show of bravado in front of this odd and frightening character, so they intentionally bump into him and send him spinning.

"Ruffians, the whole lot of you. Out of my way!" Coppélius shouts; but his anger only encourages them, and the youngsters encircle the indignant old man.

"We thought you'd like to have a little drink with us," they tease, darting this way and that, out of reach of the doctor's flailing walking stick.

In the melee, a key drops unnoticed to the ground from Coppélius's pocket. The boys finally tire of their game and leave the square, and the confused old gentleman goes on his way.

Once again the courtyard is quiet, but not for long. Figures emerge from the shadows, and Swanilda tiptoes across the square, closely followed by her girl friends. She looks around cautiously and then bends over and peeks through Dr. Coppélius's keyhole.

"Swanilda! Look what I've found!" One of her friends waves the lost key.

"What luck!" Swanilda declares. "I'm going in, and if you're true friends, you'll follow."

The girls join hands and, terrified of what Dr. Coppélius might do if he finds them, form a line behind Swanilda. She opens the door and leads them inside.

Franz, meanwhile, has plans of his own, and from behind one of the houses he appears carrying a heavy ladder. He glances at Swanilda's house and, convinced that she is asleep, leans the ladder against Coppélia's window. He begins to climb.

"My key! Where's my key?" a scratchy voice shouts into the night air.

Franz stops dead.

"Thief!" Dr. Coppélius screams.

Franz jumps from the ladder and runs off. Dr. Coppélius notices a ray of light coming from his front door and hurries into the house, closing the door behind him.

Franz reappears, tiptoeing across the square. This time, he places the ladder against a back window, determined, if Swanilda won't have him, to win the heart of the mysterious Coppélia.

Act II

Strange tools and machinery hang from the rafters of Dr. Coppélius's dark, enchanted workshop. On the right side of the room is a wooden table with a skull and candlesticks, and to the left a curtained alcove. Musty old books occupy every available surface. The girls enter, their legs shaking so much they can hardly walk. As their eyes adjust to the dim light, they have their first awful shock—they are not alone. All round the room, casting huge, black shadows on the walls, are the most bizarre figures the girls have ever seen.

"Life-size dolls!" Swanilda exclaims. "Scary old Dr. Coppélius is just a toymaker. Look, there's a Chinaman, and an astronomer, and a clown with a drum. And over there is a señorita, and a Scotsman, and a sultan."

Swanilda looks at the curtained alcove and slowly walks toward it. Swallowing hard, she pulls the red curtain back, and a chair, with Coppélia sitting on it, slides out.

Swanilda jumps. "H-h-hello, I'm Swanilda," she stammers.

Silence is the only answer.

She shakes Coppélia's ruffled skirt, but the figure on the chair doesn't move.

Swanilda puts her ear to the girl's heart and listens.

"I don't believe it!"

"What is it?" her friends ask.

"Look at this." Swanilda holds Coppélia's arm high up in the air and lets go. The arm falls lifelessly to Coppélia's side. "My foolish Franz loves a mechanical doll." And with a mischievous grin she coaxes, "Let's have some fun!"

Swanilda's friends know just what she has in mind, and they run from doll to doll, turning switches and wheels to set the bodies in motion. The clown hammers out a beat on his drum, and the room soon buzzes with the whirring of the mechanisms.

Without warning, Dr. Coppélius returns to find his workshop in chaos, his precious dolls in disarray.

"What is the meaning of this? You naughty children, can't you see you're ruining my creations?"

The frightened girls scatter about the room and, one by one, escape through the open door—all but Swanilda, who hides with Coppélia behind the red curtain.

The old man shuffles around his messy workshop and sets each toppled doll aright. When he has finished, he sits down wearily at the table, but there is no rest for him tonight. Franz, who thinks the doctor is still out, has scaled the ladder and crawls in through an open window. Dr. Coppélius rises quietly from his chair and follows the boy across the dimly lit room, imitating his every movement. Franz, sensing his presence, turns around suddenly.

"How dare you sneak into my workshop? I'll get you for this, you impudent boy!" Forgetting his advanced age, the old fellow, panting and perspiring, chases after Franz.

"But, Dr. Coppélius," Franz pleads, as he runs out of reach, "I love your daughter. Can't I see her for just a moment?"

Coppélius stops dead in his tracks and smiles slyly. "Why, of course, Franz. I'm sorry I misunderstood your intentions. But first, won't you have some of my homemade wine?"

They sit down at the table and toast Coppélia's beauty. The doctor only pretends to drink the wine, which he has drugged, but he urges Franz to drink more and more.

"I feel very tired," Franz mumbles, and collapses on the table.

Again the old man smiles. With demonic intensity, he leafs through a huge book of magic and, finding the right page, reads the formula for transferring the life force.

Dr. Coppélius goes to the window alcove and brings out his beautiful doll. But he fails to realize it is not Coppélia—it is Swanilda, who has disguised herself in the doll's clothes. The doctor intends to cast a spell on Franz, transfer the boy's life force to Coppélia's body, and thus turn his dearest possession into a human being. But Coppélius's magic will do no harm to Franz, because this "doll" is already a living, breathing person.

Dr. Coppélius brings out his beautiful doll. But he fails to realize it is not Coppélia.

Reciting the magic chant, the old man casts his spell. He gathers the energy from Franz's legs and transfers it to "Coppélia." Swanilda stiffly rises and marches mechanically on flat feet, her knees locked tight as if she had no joints, her arms extended in front, her head bobbing from side to side. Dr. Coppélius is delighted, for he believes his spell is working. He now transfers the sight from Franz's eyes to "Coppélia's." She focuses her eyes, and the first thing she does with her new vision is rap the doctor on the head. Not expecting such a response, Coppélius consults his book and realizes he has one more task to accomplish: Coppélia must have a heart.

The doctor reads the appropriate passage in his sorcery book and, with a wave of his hands, he draws out Franz's heart and bestows it on the doll. Swanilda responds like a person waking up to life from a long sleep. Dr. Coppélius is so happy to see this transformation that he sinks to his knees and weeps for joy. "Coppélia" tenderly examines the dolls in the room, as if seeing them for the first time. When she comes to Franz, she touches her hand to her heart and begs the doctor to wake him, but Coppélius adamantly refuses. Swanilda wants to get Franz out of the workshop before Dr. Coppélius gives him more magic potions, and when she doesn't get her way, she throws a tantrum. Drawing the sultan's sword, she threatens the other dolls and Coppélius himself.

The old man is horrified to see that his obedient doll has turned into a willful girl. As a last resort, he places the señorita's mantilla around her shoulders and gives her a fan, thinking these will distract her. Unable to resist a little fun, Swanilda does a Spanish dance. Dr. Coppélius is so proud of her and his astonishing creative powers that he gives her the Scotsman's plaid and watches her do a dashing Scottish jig.

The potion is wearing off, and Franz now awakens. Coppélius, eager to be rid of him, forces the lad toward the window. Behind the doctor's back, Swanilda turns the switches on all the dolls, causing a deafening racket, and triumphantly pulls the undressed body of the "real" Coppélia from the alcove.

Franz is confused, but the truth finally sinks in. "Swanilda, what a fool I've been! I've been chasing a doll with enamel eyes, when a real woman is the one I truly love."

Coppélia ACT II

Franz picks up Swanilda and carries her out of the doctor's workshop. The old man is left alone, pathetically clutching the lifeless body of Coppélia.

Act III

The town square is decorated for the festival of the bell and filled with the friends and family of the bridal couple. Swanilda and Franz, dressed in their wedding finery, have stopped quarreling at last.

The mayor presides over the ceremonies.

"Swanilda and Franz, the whole town is happy for you. Here is your dowry."

"Just one minute," shouts an angry Dr. Coppélius. "These two children have ransacked my laboratory and should be treated like criminals, not richly rewarded."

The crowd is indignant. "Go away, Coppélius. It's their wedding day."

"No, wait," says Swanilda. "Dr. Coppélius is right. I did make a mess of things." She turns to the old man. "Please take my dowry. It should pay for repairs, and perhaps you can even fix Coppélia."

"What a generous act! But the town will compensate Dr. Coppélius," the mayor decrees. "You and Franz may keep your bag of gold."

Dr. Coppélius accepts a purse from the mayor and jingles the coins absentmindedly. His anger has abated, but his sorrow at losing a "live" daughter still shows on his face.

The wedding ceremony begins, and even the sad old doctor is willing to join in a toast to the bride and groom. Swanilda and Franz look on happily as their friends dance for them. Inviting his wife to dance, Franz leads Swanilda to the center of the square. The music reflects the tenderness they feel for one another, and when Franz lifts Swanilda high in the air, she knows she is secure in his arms.

The music infects everyone, and the festival ends with the villagers dancing merrily in the descending twilight. Swanilda and Franz take their honored position in front of the crowd and, as the mayor salutes them, they joyously embrace.

— the curtain falls —

Don Quixote

Prologue

An ailing Don Quixote lies in bed surrounded by his cherished books of chivalry. His servants, imagining him near death, mourn at his bedside and then decide to throw his books into the fire to try to cure him of his mad obsession with the valiant deeds of knighthood. In his delirium, Don Quixote rises from his bed to protect his precious books and attacks his servants with a sword. As he wildly brandishes the weapon, he accidentally knocks some books off a shelf. Opening one, he is drawn into his favorite tale of romance. The beautiful Dulcinea, swathed in sea-green veils, emerges from its pages and beckons the old man; but before he can reach her, monsters appear and threaten Dulcinea. In order to rescue her, Don Quixote lunges at the imaginary giants, only to collapse exhausted on his bed.

While the Don sleeps, a fat, clumsy peasant named Sancho Panza runs into the house, pursued by three angry market women. The four of them tumble around the bedroom, creating a terrible disturbance. The Don rises from his bed, pale as a ghost, and stabs the air with his sword. Terrified, the women flee, leaving Sancho Panza to beg the Don for mercy.

"I only stole the goose to feed my poor hungry belly. I have no money, and I was starving to death." Sancho Panza's fat stomach betrays him, but nevertheless the magnanimous Don bows courteously to him.

"You are forgiven. Now you will knight me Don Quixote de la Mancha."

A very confused Sancho Panza, relieved to be spared, taps the kneeling Don on the shoulder with his sword. Following Don Quixote's orders, Sancho Panza then dresses him in a suit of armor. "And now, my loyal squire, we shall set out on our adventures," commands Don Quixote.

Fearing he has no choice, the bewildered peasant follows the knight-errant.

Act I

In a sunny courtyard in Barcelona, Kitri, the innkeeper's pretty daughter, dances in the center of a bustling crowd. Basil, a young barber who is in love with Kitri, enters the square. He serenades her with his guitar, but the free-spirited Kitri flirts with another man. Basil, in retaliation, woos a group of willing girls. Kitri's and Basil's jealous rivalry ends when the lively music slows to a romantic ballad and the young lovers dance together tenderly. As the cheering crowd gathers around them, the carnival music sounds again, and the happy couple dance gaily.

Kitri's father, Lorenzo, enters the courtyard to find his daughter in the arms of Basil. He becomes furious.

"Get away from my daughter!"

"Please, sir, I want to marry her."

"What good is it to have a poor barber like you in my family? Don Gamache wants to marry her too, and *he* is a wealthy nobleman."

"But if I'm your son-in-law, you can have a free shave every morning!"

The nobleman Don Gamache, a vain peacock in ruffles, velvets, and three-inch heels, prances into the square, waving a lace handkerchief. Lorenzo drags his protesting daughter to meet Don Gamache, but Kitri shows she has a mind of her own.

"Charmed," purrs Gamache, fanning himself with his scented handkerchief.

"I'll never marry you! Out of my sight!" she cries, shoving him away in disgust.

"Isn't she splendid?" marvels the smitten suitor, as Kitri rejoins the frolicking townsfolk.

Kitri's friends are dancing and playing their tambourines when the matadors arrive. Espada, the most famous bullfighter in Barcelona, performs a passionate fandango with Mercedes, the beautiful street dancer. In a mock bullfight, Mercedes pretends she is a bull charging toward Espada's red cape.

In the midst of all the dancing and excitement, Don Quixote, followed by his squire, rides his tired, bony horse into the square. Sancho Panza feebly blows his horn to announce his master's arrival.

Don Quixote ACT I

He gives chase, only to be accosted by their irate
boy friends, who catch poor Sancho Panza and
toss him into the air.

"Don Quixote de la Mancha at your service," says the knight and promptly falls off his horse, but he rises from the ground with noble dignity. In the meantime, Sancho Panza is grabbed and blindfolded by the village girls, who jeer and laugh as he stumbles on the cobblestones.

"Mercy!" cries Sancho, thinking vicious outlaws are molesting him.

The giggling tormentors kiss Sancho and undo his blindfold. When he discovers they are young girls, not desperadoes, he gives chase, only to be accosted by their irate boy friends, who catch poor Sancho Panza and toss him into the air. Don Quixote, seeing his loyal squire in need of assistance, charges into the fray with his jousting sword and saves Sancho.

Don Quixote, who has been admiring the lovely Kitri, decides that he has found in her his Dulcinea, the heroine of his chivalrous tales, and invites her to dance. As Kitri and the Don perform a stately waltz, Basil and Don Gamache are forced to find other partners.

After the waltz, the music grows lively. Basil and Kitri are reunited, but not for long.

"Come on, Basil, give us a dance," plead two gypsy girls.

Without a second thought, Basil happily obliges.

"Why, that good-for-nothing barber! I'll show him!" thinks Kitri, and so she does by dancing a flamenco with the handsome matadors.

Basil finally returns to dance with his willful sweetheart, lifting her high in the air to the rhythm of clapping hands. In the merriment, the accident-prone trio of Lorenzo, Sancho Panza, and Don Gamache somersault over benches and tables. While they are distracted, Kitri, determined to use the opportunity to flee from Gamache and their impending marriage, sneaks away with Basil.

"My child is gone!" curses Lorenzo.

"My bride is gone!" laments Gamache, pressing his handkerchief to his brow.

And the two, enraged by her disappearance, leave in pursuit of the runaways.

Don Quixote turns to Sancho Panza. "Loyal squire, we too shall follow my dear Dulcinea to the ends of the earth." And off they go.

Act II

SCENE 1

Kitri and Basil have wandered into a gypsy camp, set on an open plain. It is cold, and they huddle together for comfort. A windmill towers over them, silhouetted against the moonlit sky. Now that they are alone, Basil devotes himself to his sweetheart. As he gathers her in his arms, Kitri lifts over her head a long scarf, which billows like a ship's sail in the wind.

In exchange for Kitri's ring, the gypsies have given the young couple a change of clothes as a disguise. When Don Gamache and Lorenzo approach the camp, the gypsies attack them, temporarily diverting the two pursuers from their search.

No sooner are Don Gamache and Lorenzo driven off than Don Quixote and Sancho Panza stumble into the camp. The gypsies all bow to the illustrious knight and begin dancing. Basil enters disguised as a gypsy, followed by a veiled Kitri, and they set up a little stage. The gypsy children take their seats, and a puppet show begins. Suddenly a loud voice rings out from the back of the audience.

"Stop at once! Stop, I say!" Don Quixote, losing himself in the fantasy of the play, believes his Dulcinea is in danger and storms the puppet theater. Then, thinking the sails of the windmill are monstrous giants, the fearless knight charges.

"Come back, sir! You're outnumbered!" pleads his squire.

But before Sancho Panza can stop him, Don Quixote is caught up on one of the windmill's sails, carried into the air, and thrown to the ground.

SCENE 2

Unconscious from his fall, the wounded Don Quixote is visited by a dream. To a haunting melody, a veiled Dulcinea, the image of Kitri, floats toward him, and the Queen of the Dryads leads her wood nymphs into his dreamscape. Amor, the spirit of love, presides over the romantic reverie. One by one, Dulcinea, Amor, and the Queen perform for the Don. After their elegant solos, the wood nymphs return to join the three in a final dance before the night ends and the Don's dream fades.

Don Quixote ACT II, Scene 2

Act III

SCENE 1

Kitri and Basil have taken shelter in a nearby tavern. As the afternoon draws to a close, we find them celebrating with three friends. Still on their trail, Don Gamache and Lorenzo arrive at the tavern, followed closely by Don Quixote and Sancho Panza. Basil and Kitri hide under a tablecloth, but Lorenzo soon spots his runaway child.

"Get out from under that table or I'll drag you out!"

"I won't!" shouts the defiant Kitri.

While Basil makes his escape, Kitri's father grabs her by the arm and pulls; but Kitri is being tugged in the other direction by her friends. Basil, wrapped in a cloak, returns to the chaotic scene and stands before Lorenzo.

"I'd rather die than live without your daughter!"

Basil pretends to plunge a razor into his heart, drops his cloak, and collapses. In turn, Kitri, aware of Basil's plan, pretends to faint. When she comes to, she grabs the razor and sobs. She then tries to revive her supposedly dying sweetheart by placing a bottle of wine to his lips.

"Basil, speak to me!" she cries, bending over him to hear his heartbeat. Aware that no one is looking, Basil sneaks a kiss.

Don Quixote, who believes in the sanctity of love, demands that Lorenzo allow the couple to marry before they are parted by death. As Lorenzo reluctantly offers his blessing, Don Quixote tries to convince Don Gamache to accept the dictates of true love.

The spoiled Gamache stamps and rages. "Draw your sword, you old fool!"

But the silly aristocrat is no better at swordplay than the tired old knight. Don Quixote spears Gamache's wig, claims it as his trophy, and the duel is over. Then, to everyone's amazement, Basil miraculously recovers.

SCENE 2

Gypsies, bridesmaids, family, and friends dance under twinkling lanterns at the wedding party of Basil and Kitri. To a lyric melody, the lovers perform an elegant pas de deux. Basil escorts Kitri to the center of the square, where she spins in his arms. Basil's dancing is strong and powerful, as befits his new station in life as Kitri's husband, and Kitri, happy finally to have the man she loves, dances gaily.

Lorenzo has become reconciled to their marriage, and congratulates them heartily. As the crowd dances, the proud father invites Don Quixote to partner his daughter, but the old knight refuses: he now sees that Kitri is not his longed-for Dulcinea. When Dulcinea's gossamer vision beckons him, the Don, bewitched again, follows. Accompanied by the loyal Sancho Panza, Don Quixote de la Mancha departs once more on his quest for truth and beauty.

— the curtain falls —

Basil escorts Kitri to the center of the square, where she spins in his arms.

La Fille Mal Gardée

Act I

Dawn is breaking over the Widow Simone's sleepy farmyard. A rooster and his hens shake out their feathers, and, as the sun rises, the birds strut around the barnyard, scratching and kicking.

Pretty Lise, the wealthy widow's only daughter, tiptoes out of the house and runs down the steep farmhouse stairs to look for her beau, the handsome farmer Colas. She hears her mother opening the shutters and hurriedly looks for a place to hide.

"I'd better wait under the balcony or she's sure to call me to my chores," Lise thinks.

The widow emerges from the house, dressed in her nightcap and gown, and shakes a dusty blanket over the balcony right onto poor Lise's head.

"Oh no!" Lise mutters, brushing off her dress.

After her mother goes back into the house, Lise strolls to the barn and pours herself a bowl of cream. She lazily licks the spoon, dreaming of her true love. She ties her long pink sash on the barn door in a lovers' knot and goes into the house.

Moments later, an equally lovestruck Colas arrives, looking for his sweetheart. He doesn't dare knock on her door, for the Widow Simone is not happy about their romance and does her best to keep them apart.

"Lise has been thinking of me already," Colas murmurs when he notices the sash. "Ah, what a fine morning!"

He ties the ribbon to his staff and prances around the yard, leaping joyously to the rousing music. Mounting the stairs to the balcony, he peers through the

La Fille Mal Gardée ACT I

shutters, hoping to catch a glimpse of his love. Instead, he is knocked down the steps by a firm blow to the nose as Widow Simone opens the shutters.

"What do you want?" she demands.

"May I see Lise?"

"You? Never!" She stalks back inside.

"What's all this noise?" Lise wonders as she emerges from the door below.

"Lise, my love!" Colas cries, and kisses her.

Lise is delighted to see Colas, but the old widow, curlers and clips still in her hair, scurries out of the house and chases him away. She spanks Lise and hands her a broom.

"Now start sweeping, you bad girl," she orders.

Lise is all the more embarrassed by this treatment because her friends, the harvesters, have begun to arrive in the barnyard. The widow distributes scythes for the day's work, and the merry group sets off for the fields. Lise, eager to find Colas, tries to steal away with the harvesters.

"Oh no you don't!" her mother scolds, dragging her to a bench. "You're going to sit here and churn butter."

As the Widow Simone goes to the barn for the churn, Colas sneaks unnoticed into the yard. He lifts Lise high over his head, hugs her happily, and then runs up the ladder to hide in the hayloft.

"I want you to watch me so you'll do this correctly," says Lise's mother when she returns. In her zeal to demonstrate the art of making butter, Madame Simone pushes on the paddle so hard that the churn crashes down on her toe.

"Ouch! Ouch! Ouch!" she squeals, and hobbles into the house.

Giggling, Lise returns to her post, but she cannot concentrate on the butter. All she can think of is her sweetheart.

"Psst! Lise, let's escape while she's inside," whispers Colas, who has climbed down the ladder.

"I want to go, but I have work to do."

Disappointed, Colas turns to leave the yard, but Lise, noticing her ribbon tied to his staff, stops him. She takes the ribbon and tenderly binds his hands with it.

"If you untie me, I'll churn the butter for you," he coaxes.

Colas sets to work, but soon they are kissing and hugging instead. He finds a longer ribbon on the bench and tosses one end to his sweetheart. Lise catches it, and Colas winds himself in the ribbon into her arms. When he unwinds himself, Lise has a turn, twirling into Colas's embrace. To a sweet melody, Lise and Colas now play cat's cradle with the ribbon, forming a love knot of crisscrossing patterns. They kiss again but are interrupted by Lise's girl friends. Colas flees, and Lise runs back to the butter churn.

"Come dance with us," the girls beg.

Lise and Colas now play cat's cradle with the ribbon, forming a love knot of crisscrossing patterns.

Lise and her friends dance merrily about the farmyard to a gay tune, spinning exuberantly on this lovely morning. Suddenly the kitchen door flies open and out waddles Simone, dressed in her Sunday best.

"Come into the house, Lise. It's time to change your clothes. Monsieur Thomas and his son, Alain, are coming to pay their respects and discuss your marriage contract. Ah, we shall be even richer when we join our farm to their great vineyards."

"No! I won't marry Alain and you can't make me!"

Simone shoos the girls away and then pulls Lise across her knees for a proper spanking. It is in this awkward position that Monsieur Thomas and Master Alain find them.

"We didn't expect you so soon," says the embarrassed widow. "Lise, curtsy like a good girl."

Lise shyly obeys.

"Now go into the house, child, while we discuss an important matter," Simone coos sweetly.

Thomas introduces Alain to the old widow. Never has there been such a clumsy, foolish young suitor. Alain's freckled face is flushed with embarrassment. His velvet coat is buttoned tightly over his narrow chest, and a childish feathered cap perches on his yellow tufts of hair. He clutches a red umbrella and looks like an overgrown baby.

"Hello," he squeaks and drops to the ground, concealing himself behind his open umbrella. The widow watches in amazement as Alain and the umbrella roll away across the yard.

Thomas, patting his big belly with fatherly pride, offers Madame Simone a share of his vineyards if Lise will marry his son. Madame readily agrees, and he presents her with two large bags of gold to seal the bargain. Meanwhile, the childish Alain is riding his umbrella like a hobby horse around the farmyard.

Lise, in a pretty new dress, rejoins them and, at his father's request, Alain offers her a flower.

"Mama," she whispers, "he makes me sick."

"Sssh, child! Sit here while Alain dances for us, and hold your tongue."

Alain is so bowlegged that his feet barely meet. With his stiff arms flying, he jerks his ungainly legs this way and that, finally somersaulting forward into

Thomas's and Simone's laps. Lise narrowly escapes, jumping out of his reach, but before she has a chance to flee the yard, Monsieur Thomas's horse and cart arrive to carry the ladies to the harvest. Mother and daughter, in their summer bonnets, drive off in the carriage, while Thomas and his silly son trot cheerfully behind, trailed by the bright, sunny music.

Act II

The hens and rooster swagger along a path that leads through the woods to the wheatfields. Monsieur Thomas's carriage soon appears on the path, with Alain galloping behind on his umbrella. Unable to maintain a steady course, the clumsy Alain canters into a group of village girls, becomes hopelessly entangled in their flying streamers, and is swept along to the harvest.

Colas, a bottle of wine in each hand, is eager to meet Lise at the harvest festivities. He jumps for joy, while a spirited tune plays, and hurries along a shortcut to the fields,

*   *   *

The harvesters are finishing their work when Colas arrives with the wine. The girls form a circle around him and dance, but they are interrupted by the entrance of Monsieur Thomas and his party. After stepping down from the carriage, Simone whispers a few words to Monsieur Thomas, and the two conspirators encourage shy Alain to ask Lise for a dance. Lise has no choice but to accept, but while she dances with Alain, Colas appears at her side.

"Hello, my love," he whispers and sneaks a kiss and a hug at every opportunity. Alain, absorbed in his performance, doesn't notice a thing.

Well aware of Lise's preference, her girl friends distract Alain. "Dance with us!" "We deserve a turn," they coax. Flattered, Alain obliges, and the sweethearts are left with each other.

Under Colas's admiring gaze, Lise leaps and spins through the air. He hands her eight long ribbons, which she holds aloft. Each of Lise's girl friends grasps the end of a ribbon, and they skip around her as if she were a maypole. Then the girls create lovely crisscrossing patterns with the ribbons as the lovers dance. The romantic serenade fades, and a lively tune accompanies Colas as he displays his excitement with spectacular turns around the field. Lise dances toward him, and he lifts her high into the air.

Madame Simone discovers Lise and Colas embracing.

"Every time my back is turned, this is what goes on!"

Luckily, Lise is saved from further scolding when a friend offers Madame Simone a pair of wooden clogs and persuades her to join in a clog dance. With great bravura, she clicks her heels together and taps along to the playful melody. Four graceful village girls accompany her, clapping their hands and rising onto the toes of their wooden shoes. Madame Simone tries to imitate them, but, unable to keep her balance, she slips and slides across the field as if it were an icy pond. To the delight of her partners, she invents her own outrageous steps, and everyone applauds wildly.

The boys carry a maypole to the center of the field and all the harvesters dance around it, holding onto the colorful ribbons and weaving an interlacing pattern at the crown.

The celebration is in full swing when suddenly the sky darkens and lightning flashes. Soon the wind is blowing furiously, rocking the maypole and tossing the merrymakers this way and that. Simone sees Alain fly by with his umbrella and grabs hold of him for protection from the rain. The force of the storm sends Monsieur Thomas crashing into Simone, and, huddled together, the two watch in awe as the wind catches Alain's umbrella and carries him up and away into the clouds.

Act III

"Mama, do you need help?" asks Lise, entering the farmhouse with a heavy sheaf of wheat on her shoulders. Simone stumbles behind, doubled over from the weight of her enormous load. Lise assists her mother and then watches in horror as Simone locks the front door and deposits the key in her apron pocket.

"I'm going to keep you under my eye long enough to see you married to Alain. Now come and help me with the spinning."

Lise resigns herself to imprisonment. As Simone spins, Lise plays out the thread. Soon she is unwinding faster than Simone can spin, until the widow finds herself bound and almost strangled by yarn. Lise disentangles her mother, who sinks back exhausted. Simone yawns and closes her eyes. Resourceful Lise tries to sneak the key from her mother's pocket, but the old woman, only half asleep, stops her.

Simone, realizing she must stay awake and watchful, takes a tambourine from a shelf and asks Lise to dance. Lise does a jig as Simone plays the tambourine, but the tired old widow soon begins to yawn and falls asleep again.

Meanwhile, Colas scales the outside wall, opens the window above the front door, and peers in. Lise runs to the door and raises her arms. Without entering the room, he lifts her high in the air, and she swings from his arms like a pendulum.

Simone stirs. Abruptly releasing Lise, Colas slams the window and drops out of sight. Simone, half awake, half asleep, claps her hands in time to the jig, and Lise quickly begins to dance, but now her steps are awkward and confused.

"Lise, you're acting strangely. Is anything wrong?" asks Simone, feeling her daughter's forehead.

Lise shakes her head, and the two dance merrily together. When a knock startles them, Simone answers the door to find the farmboys carrying her sheaves of wheat. Concealed among the bundles, Colas smuggles himself into the house. Simone distributes coins to the harvesters, who dance in celebration.

Lise thinks, "I must escape now or I'll be married off to Alain."

She joins the dance, and the boys lift her high over their heads. They are about to carry her out through the door when Simone springs to attention and pulls her daughter back.

The clock strikes, reminding the widow that she has an appointment with Thomas to make the final arrangements for the wedding. As she leaves the house, she locks the door behind her.

"You can't keep me prisoner!" shrieks Lise. "It's not fair!" The poor girl huddles on the couch, pouting and crying, until thoughts of a future life with Colas console her. Pretending she is dressed in her wedding gown, Lise walks down a make-believe aisle and exchanges vows with her groom. She is in the middle of mothering five imaginary little children when Colas jumps out from the pile of wheat.

"Oh no!" she cries. "You heard everything." Lise blushes in embarrassment and confusion, but Colas is delighted to know how much she loves him. He dries her tears with his kerchief and exchanges his scarf for hers. As they embrace, Lise spies her mother through the window, trotting homeward.

"You must hide before she comes in! Quick, under here." She pulls him to the table. "No, here!" and she shoves him into the fireplace. "It's no use, she's bound to find you. I know—in my bedroom."

They are up the stairs in a flash, Lise pushing Colas through the bedroom door and slamming it behind him.

The flustered girl runs down the stairs and begins sweeping the floor busily as Simone enters the house.

"What's wrong with you today? The house is clean. You must be ill." Again the widow feels Lise's forehead. "Wait a minute, that's not your scarf! It's Colas's! Where is he?" She searches every nook and cranny. "If you won't confess, I'm going to lock you in your room."

Simone drags Lise upstairs and pushes her into the bedroom. "And make sure you change your dress. It's almost time for your wedding."

Hearing a knock, Simone runs down the stairs and with great ceremony greets Monsieur Thomas and the notary. The notary has drawn up the marriage papers to the satisfaction of both Simone and Thomas; with quill pens they sign on the dotted line.

"This is a happy day, Madame," beams Thomas.

"Let's drink to that, Monsieur," Simone replies, and they clink their glasses. The guests enter the house, followed by the bridegroom, who clutches his umbrella in one hand and a big diamond ring in the other. Thomas, Simone, and the notary link arms and dance while Alain leaps around the floor like a prancing kangaroo.

"Now, Alain," commands Simone. "Take the key and claim your bride." She points to the upstairs bedroom.

"B-b-but, I c-c-can't," he stutters.

"Yes, you can!" the crowd cheers.

He slowly climbs the stairs, pausing at every step. When he finally reaches the top, he hesitates.

"Go on!" the crowd encourages him.

Alain turns the key and opens the door. There before him, dressed in her wedding gown, stands Lise, wrapped in the arms of another man. In shock,

La Fille Mal Gardée ACT II

Alain stumbles backward down the stairs. Simone faints. Monsieur Thomas flies into a rage. And arm in arm, Lise and Colas descend the staircase.

Lise pleads with her mother. "He's the only man I'll ever love. Won't you accept Colas as your son-in-law?"

Simone sobs but nods her head. "It's the only way to keep her out of trouble. What else can I do?"

"It's easy enough to rip up one contract and draw up another," the notary volunteers, and while he shreds the marriage papers an indignant Monsieur Thomas pulls his simple son out through the door.

Colas kisses Madame Simone's hand, and the wealthy widow, won over at last, embraces him heartily. The guests settle down to watch the bridal couple dance, and the house vibrates with joy and affection. Colas and Lise perform a romantic duet as their friends toss confetti in the air. Then everyone links hands to form a long chain which winds its way out of the door, over the hills, and into the fields.

All is quiet. Alain seizes this opportunity to sneak back into the house through an open window. He scans the room.

"There it is!" he cries, and, hugging his beloved umbrella to his chest, he scampers out again.

— the curtain falls —

"There it is!" Alain cries, and, hugging his beloved umbrella to his chest, he scampers out again.

Firebird

Scene I

A golden apple tree grows within the walled garden of the evil magician Kastchei. The Firebird, attracted by the gleaming fruit, flies into the garden. In the background, a forbidding melody rumbles like an approaching storm, warning trespassers of danger.

Ivan Tsarevitch, a young Russian prince, peers over the wall at the golden tree and discovers the Firebird. He climbs the wall and aims his crossbow at the marvelous bird as she darts past him, her feathers blazing red and orange. Blinded by her brilliant plumage, Ivan is unable to shoot, and he hides to wait for a better opportunity. When the creature stands still, he aims again, but the Firebird catches sight of him and flees. Ivan retreats to the shadows.

Thinking him gone, the Firebird returns to dance. She is a magnificent creature, strong and beautiful—the most exotic being the simple prince has ever seen. He recognizes how special she is, and no longer wishes to destroy her.

"But I must capture her," he thinks.

As she reaches for a golden apple, the prince seizes her. The Firebird is terrified and at first remains motionless, but then, in a frantic attempt to free herself, she flutters her arms wildly. Gently restraining them, Ivan tries to reassure the agitated Firebird. Praying that he intends her no harm, she slowly relaxes. Ivan pulls her toward him and, hoping she will trust him, loosens his hold. The Firebird stands quietly. Ivan lifts her high above his head, and she waves her arms as if in flight. As the flutes play an exotic melody, conjuring up visions of the Orient, they dance.

"Now will you give me my freedom?" she begs, her body bent in submission.

"If that is what you wish," Ivan answers.

As he frees her, she plucks a feather from her breast and presents it to the prince.

"Take this. It will call me to your side if ever trouble finds you."

Tucking the magic feather in his pocket, Ivan watches in awe as the Firebird flies away.

Ivan now senses a new presence in this enchanted garden and hides once again. Like visions in a dream, twelve beautiful maidens dressed in white emerge from the shadows. They pose silently for a moment and then form two lines, creating a passageway for the loveliest of all, Princess Unearthly Beauty. She, along with her attendants, is held captive by evil Kastchei the Immortal. Ivan, hypnotized by the princess's loveliness, watches silently as the maidens gather golden apples from the tree and toss them about in the moonlight. The night breezes rustle their skirts, and the music is comforting.

Dancing alone, surrounded by her friends, the princess takes her turn to toss an apple in the air. Prince Ivan boldly steps forward to catch it. She stares at him wide-eyed, then backs away, shy and afraid.

Removing his cap, Ivan bows. "Please don't leave. Here's your apple."

The princess accepts the apple from the handsome youth. Six maidens encircle Ivan and six surround the princess. They call to one another from their separate circles and then move closer, each with six attendants in tow. At first the maidens hold them back, but they finally allow the two to meet. At last Princess Unearthly Beauty dances for Ivan and he finds her irresistible. With a kiss, their love is sealed.

A trumpet call pierces the night. Faint at first, it grows louder, sounding its cry again and again. The music quickens, urgently summoning the captive maidens, and they flee in fear for their safety. The princess runs after them.

"Why do you run? What danger are you in?" Ivan calls to her.

"You musn't follow. Beware of the evil that lies here. Kastchei, our master, will turn you to stone if you trespass further. Farewell."

She disappears through the castle gates, which close fast behind her.

Firebird SCENE I

Scene II

Ivan's love has made him fearless. Determined to follow the princess, he pulls on the gates with all his might. As the music increases in fury, the gates fly open, unleashing a swarm of horrible monsters, slaves of the evil Kastchei. In terror, Ivan dashes for the garden wall, but Kastchei's soldiers seize him before he can escape. As they hold him, members of the captive court enter the garden.

Suddenly the deformed and hideous beasts prostrate themselves on the ground, and soldiers, swordsmen, and harem girls bow low. Kastchei the Immortal enters the garden. He is a living skeleton, supporting his ancient bones with a walking stick. Ivan stares with apprehension at Kastchei's long white hair and beard, his majestic crown, his royal cloak. Beckoning with his terrible claws, Kastchei calls Ivan to him, and the prince reluctantly inches forward.

"The Firebird will protect me," he suddenly remembers. "I have nothing to fear."

Prince Ivan faces the horrible Kastchei and spits at him in disgust. The Immortal One is enraged. Kastchei's followers curse the prince and demons jump on his back. As Ivan stands, restrained and helpless, the princess and her handmaidens enter the garden and beseech their master to spare him.

"Never! I shall turn him to stone on this very spot!" howls Kastchei.

Ivan wrests his arms free from his captors and, pulling the magic feather from his pocket, waves it in the air. Instantly, the Firebird flies into the garden, and within seconds she has all of Kastchei's monsters whirling in circles. As she dances in the center of their mad spinning, the music grows fiercer. Everyone in

Kastchei is a living skeleton, supporting his ancient bones with a walking stick.

Kastchei's power—soldiers, demons, and slaves—dances to the Firebird's command. Even the poor maidens and their princess are drawn into the frenzy. With feet pounding and heads bowed, the captive court is driven by the urgent music. Helpless to interfere, Kastchei watches his subjects bend to the will of the Firebird and sink to the ground. Finally, even the great Kastchei is forced to his knees.

The Firebird, alone in the center of the fallen bodies, stands erect and majestic. She points to Kastchei and his court and orders them to rise. A sultry lullaby is heard as, one by one, the Firebird consigns them to sleep. Harem girls, soldiers, monsters, and maidens fall to the earth. Only Kastchei successfully fights to stay awake. Dancing among the prostrate court, the Firebird beckons Ivan Tsarevitch. He steps from the shadows, amazed at the scene he has witnessed.

"Hidden in a casket in that tree lies a golden egg, the source of Kastchei's power, the container of his immortal soul. Destroy that and you free the princess," the Firebird tells him.

Prince Ivan rushes to the hiding place, finds the box, and seizes the egg. Kastchei, in horror, staggers toward the prince, but before he can reach him, Ivan raises the huge egg overhead and throws it to the ground. As it shatters, so does Kastchei's immortal soul. The evil one falls dead.

Scene III

The sun shines on the spires and roofs of a brilliantly colored city. The kingdom, freed from the curse of Kastchei, prospers. Prince Ivan is to marry the Princess Unearthly Beauty today, and her handmaidens will be wed to the knights of the Russian court. The music resounds triumphantly as the royal procession gathers.

Dressed in their coronation robes, Prince Ivan and his bride are declared Tsar and Tsarina of Holy Russia. Ivan raises his scepter high to a cheering throng and expresses the hope and exhilaration of his people embarking on a bright new future.

—the curtain falls—

53

Kastchei's followers curse the prince and demons jump on his back.

Giselle

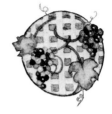

Act I

It is harvest time in the vineyards along the Rhine. A group of peasants, laughing and swinging straw baskets, walk to the fields past the small cottage where Giselle and her mother, Berthe, live. Giselle is a delicate girl and must stay at home while her friends work in the vineyards. Hilarion, a young gamekeeper who has long loved Giselle, pauses at her door. As he is about to knock, he hears someone coming and hides behind a tree. Two men arrive and enter another cottage across the way; they are Albrecht, the Count of Silesia, and his companion, Wilfred. Albrecht is Hilarion's rival for Giselle's affections.

When the count emerges from his cottage, he has exchanged his elegant velvet cape for a leather jerkin.

"Do you think these clothes look common enough, Wilfred? I rather fancy being dressed this way."

"Count Albrecht, don't you think this disguise has gone too far?" Wilfred protests. "The girl is head over heels in love with you, and you know you'll never be able to marry her. You should be courting Bathilde, the Prince of Courland's daughter, not a country girl. Your marriage has been arranged since childhood."

"That's enough," Albrecht commands. "I shall do as I like."

"Then I beg Your Highness, if you're going to continue in this disguise, please give me your sword."

Albrecht obliges him, and Wilfred puts the sword in the cottage before withdrawing.

Giselle ACT I

Like a boy in love for the first time, Albrecht rushes to Giselle's door. He knocks and, hearing his loved one's footsteps, playfully ducks out of sight.

Giselle skips out of her house to a lilting tune, her cheeks flushed at the thought of seeing her new suitor. Although Giselle cannot see Albrecht, she can hear him blowing kisses, and she smiles with satisfaction. Knowing that her new love is watching, she dances, but still the count won't reveal himself. Then, just when she thinks he must have gone, Albrecht steps into her path. Hoping to assure Giselle of his devotion, he pledges his undying love.

"You are too quick with your vows," she says, doubting that such an unusual man could care for her. She picks a daisy from her garden and, to tender music, plucks the petals: "He loves me, he loves me not." She stops a moment, eyes shining, and looks adoringly at Albrecht. "He loves me, he loves me n—?"

Giselle realizes the remaining petals will declare her lover faithless and, weeping, she throws the flower to the ground. Albrecht rescues the daisy and secretly plucks out one more petal. He returns the flower to Giselle and urges her to continue.

"He loves me!" A smile lights up her face, and she and Albrecht dance like two carefree children.

Hilarion comes out of hiding.

"What's going on? Do you love this man?" He is violently jealous.

Giselle nods.

"No, you love me! Say it!"

He falls to his knees and pleads passionately with Giselle. Albrecht has soon had enough of this tantrum and pulls Hilarion away from her. The gamekeeper responds by drawing a knife. Albrecht instinctively reaches for his missing sword and then majestically points a finger at Hilarion, ordering him to leave. Stunned at this posturing, Hilarion notices that Albrecht's hand rests on his hip, where a nobleman's sword might be. The dawning realization that this man is not who he appears to be subdues Hilarion, and he stumbles away.

Music heralds the return of the harvesters. Their baskets are brimming with ripe grapes, which they eagerly show their beloved Giselle. Albrecht pops a grape into his mouth, enjoying this peasant romp. Giselle suggests a dance and takes her place in front of the girls, who form a backdrop for her solo. Light as a spirit, her body melts into the music. She poses in arabesque, leaning toward

Albrecht. Albrecht takes her hand, and their bodies sway toward each other as they link arms and dance. Inspired by his love, Giselle spins down a line of her admiring girl friends, her arms swinging in abandon. As the music speeds up in joyous celebration, Albrecht takes the opportunity to kiss her, which only adds fire to her already burning cheeks.

Giselle, feverish with excitement and nearly faint, is discovered by Berthe.

"Your brow is so warm. What have you been doing, my little darling?" asks her mother.

"I have been dancing!"

"Too vigorously, I'm afraid. Your weak heart cannot bear such strain."

Berthe reminds Giselle of the terrible legend of the Wilis—unfortunate maidens who are doomed to dance into eternity. She fears Giselle will dance herself to death, and ushers her daughter into the house in spite of Albrecht's protests. As the harvesters disperse, Albrecht hears the horn of the royal hunting party and runs off. He is afraid he will be discovered by his fiancée, Bathilde, and her father.

Hilarion, who has been hiding nearby, now seizes the chance to solve the mystery of his rival. He peers through the window of Albrecht's cottage and, seeing a shiny object inside, pries open the door with his knife.

"I was right," he thinks, holding up a beautiful sword engraved with the royal coat of arms of Silesia.

The sounds of the hunt draw near. Hilarion shuts the cottage door and waits inside for his opportunity to expose the impostor.

Courtly music accompanies the lavish procession. The peasants rush to the little square, marveling at the nobility's rich velvets and brocades. This is the Prince of Courland's party, and on the prince's arm is his beautiful daughter, Bathilde. Wilfred has joined the hunters and nervously scans the crowd in search of the disguised Albrecht. The Prince of Courland is thirsty and commands his squire to fetch them wine. Giselle's house is the nearest at hand, and the squire knocks on her door.

Berthe, amazed to find a royal entourage gathered at her cottage, humbly curtsies and runs to get some wine. Giselle soon emerges from the cottage bearing a pitcher.

"Good day, Your Highness. Won't you sit and quench your thirst?"

As the prince and his daughter drink their wine, Giselle is entranced by the satin brocade of Bathilde's dress. She gathers the long train in her hand and presses the cloth to her cheek. The princess jumps up, and Giselle apologizes, ashamed. Bathilde, noticing the pretty peasant girl for the first time, discovers that Giselle loves to dance, and invites her to perform for the royal party.

To a lyrical melody, Giselle raises her arms high, spins on one foot, and poses in perfect arabesque. As the melody becomes playful, her motions quicken until she finishes her dance with broad turns to the now rollicking music.

"Father, isn't she pretty? I've never seen such a charming dance," marvels Bathilde. "I shall give her my gold locket as a present."

Giselle blushingly accepts the tribute and invites the distinguished guests to rest indoors. To a courtly march, Bathilde and her father enter the cottage, followed by Berthe and Giselle. The prince's squire hangs the royal hunting horn on the door and follows the rest of the party into the forest. Wilfred goes off to find Albrecht.

With Albrecht's sword and velvet cape in hand, Hilarion now approaches Giselle's door. He finds the hunting horn and notices that it bears the same emblem as that on the sword: the royal coat of arms of the House of Silesia. Now there can be no doubt. Albrecht is an aristocrat and therefore can only be toying with Giselle's heart. Hilarion smiles with satisfaction at the thought of exposing his rival.

However, Hilarion must delay his triumph. The harvest festival is about to begin, and the village girls come dancing into the little square. The boys follow, pulling a cart decorated with the last flowers of the season and containing an enormous wine cask. Hearing all the noise, Giselle and Berthe emerge from the cottage, and Giselle is immediately crowned Queen of the Harvest. Albrecht comes out of hiding, delighted to find that his love has been awarded such an honor.

Giselle and Albrecht dance in celebration, playfully blowing kisses to one another. As Giselle watches, Albrecht leaps with majestic ease through the fallen leaves, winning the admiration of everyone—partly because of his dancing, but mostly because he makes Giselle so happy. Giselle beckons to her waiting friends to dance, and the square comes alive with the color of swirling skirts and flashing smiles.

As the dancing ends, Giselle is roughly pulled away from Albrecht by Hilarion.

"Do you love this man?" Hilarion demands.

"Yes, I love him," answers Giselle.

Hilarion retrieves Albrecht's sheathed sword from its hiding place and separates the lovers with it.

"This sword belongs to him!" Hilarion shouts.

In anger, Albrecht pulls the sword from its sheath and points it at Hilarion. Backed against Giselle's door, Hilarion seizes the horn from its hook and brings it to his lips. He calls the hunting party, and the nobles, along with the loyal Wilfred, converge on the square. Albrecht attempts to run from Giselle and his shame, but it is too late: Bathilde and her father have emerged from the house and he is trapped.

"Albrecht, why are you dressed so oddly?" Bathilde asks.

Albrecht smiles guiltily and kisses his fiancée's hand like a devoted lover. This is more than Giselle can comprehend. She violently parts Bathilde and Albrecht and stands between them, shielding Albrecht from the princess.

"This is *my* sweetheart!"

"Nonsense, child. I am engaged to this man, Albrecht, Count of Silesia."

The blow shatters Giselle's delicate heart. Yanking the locket from her neck, she casts it to the ground, her hair falling wildly about her anguished face. Berthe tries to soothe the girl, but Giselle cannot be comforted. She tears away from her mother's embrace and buries her head in her hands. Suddenly she is in the grip of madness.

Giselle looks up, but she can no longer see the friends and nobility that surround her. Slowly, she plucks an imaginary daisy's petals, one by one, as she had done so happily that morning. The same melody accompanies her actions, but now the music is tinged with melancholy. Albrecht tries to comfort her, but she is blinded by her madness and lost in her reverie of the past.

The sword, lying abandoned on the ground, draws her attention. She grasps it at the tip of the blade, and, dragging it around the square, traces an enormous circle at the feet of the horrified crowd. Berthe gasps in terror, and Hilarion, aware of her terrible intention, rushes to her side and wrests the sword from her hands.

The blow shatters Giselle's delicate heart.

Giselle's lilting theme is heard again, and she feebly re-creates the dance of love she shared with Albrecht. He now realizes what he has done: Giselle's love was a jewel, and he thought it a casual gift.

Finally, Giselle's frail heart can no longer bear the strain of her madness. She reaches out to her mother and falls into her arms like a rag doll. She turns weakly to Albrecht, her eyes filled with love and forgiveness, and she dies heartbroken.

Barely aware of what he is doing, Albrecht seizes his sword and confronts Hilarion.

"Do you see what your jealousy has wrought?" Albrecht cries.

"You were the cause of this! I was true to Giselle."

Albrecht lunges at Hilarion, but Wilfred prevents him from harming the gamekeeper.

"What's the use?" mourns Albrecht. "Revenge won't bring her back to me."

Albrecht, Hilarion, Berthe, and all the villagers weep before the body of their beloved Giselle.

Act II

A church bell chimes mournfully. It is midnight in a moonlit forest glade. Giselle's grave is marked by a simple wooden cross and surrounded by fallen leaves. Hilarion is sobbing on her tomb, aware now of the tragedy caused by his jealousy. Lightning flashes, illuminating the forest, and a frightened Hilarion runs away.

Out of the dense white mist a beautiful, ghostly figure rises. It is Myrtha, Queen of the Wilis, the keeper of the spirits of girls who, betrayed by their sweethearts, have died of a broken heart. The icy perfection of her dance speaks of a terrible vengeance, for with the help of the Wilis she traps faithless lovers and forces them to dance until death.

She gathers two myrtle branches, waves them over Giselle's grave, and then solemnly tosses them into the woods. White specters rise from their bed of leaves, the moonlight glowing through their gowns, and encircle their queen like ghostly bridesmaids.

At Myrtha's command, the Wilis drop to their knees, bowing in rhythmic motion. With perfect grace, they dance a partnerless waltz.

Myrtha soars high above the glade to a gay carnival tune, her cold bearing contradicting the music. As the tempo accelerates, the girls stand in rows on either side of the clearing, poised in arabesque. With heads bowed, they hop forward as their ranks increase in number, until hundreds of shadows are cast on the earth.

Myrtha beckons to her Wilis. "Tonight we initiate a new companion. Giselle, sister in suffering, come forward."

A spirit veiled in gossamer rises from the grave. The queen removes the veil, and Giselle spins like a top that has been released.

Myrtha and her handmaidens welcome their new sister, but approaching footsteps interrupt them, and they disappear into the forest.

Albrecht enters the clearing. No longer does he possess the arrogant gaze and gay smile of youth. He is pale, his brow creased with melancholy. Weeping, he brushes his cheek with the white lilies he has brought, and then places them on Giselle's grave.

The wind changes direction and the night sounds cease. Albrecht senses that Giselle is with him, but he searches the clearing in vain. Sinking to his knees, he buries his face in his hands. Giselle floats past him, and Albrecht rises and follows her vaporous trail. When at last he finds her, he is unsure whether the form he lifts is real or a dream.

The music is as ethereal as Giselle's presence, and they dance as if in heaven, their suffering behind them. The music becomes less mournful, and we know Giselle has forgiven Albrecht. She gathers the lilies and tosses them one by one into the air. Albrecht follows her footsteps and the path made by the petals deep into the woods.

With their departure, the Wilis return. They have found Hilarion wandering in the forest, and they bring him to their queen.

"I sentence you, Hilarion, as the vindictive, jealous suitor of Giselle, to dance until death."

Poor Hilarion, who really did love Giselle, is tossed about by the Wilis like a toy. The music is frantic, demonic in its intensity. The Wilis claw at him and grab his arms, pulling him back and forth in their dance of death. There is no escape, and as Hilarion gasps for breath, his captors dance on.

Hilarion begs Myrtha for mercy, but she silently points her finger, commanding him to continue his gruesome dance.

Hilarion leaps along a diagonal line that the Wilis have formed, his muscles and joints aching with fatigue. Again he begs for relief, but the force of Myrtha's wrath sends him spinning to a horrible death in the arms of his silent tormentors.

One by one, the Wilis follow their queen from the glade, and they soon return with Albrecht, their next victim. Albrecht, his eyes wide with horror, pleads with Myrtha for his life.

"Your prayers are of no use. I sentence you, disloyal lover of Giselle, to dance until death."

Giselle, entering the glade, throws herself before Albrecht to shelter him from Myrtha's lethal stare.

"Giselle, am I to die? Are you never to rest because of my betrayal?" Albrecht asks.

"The past is forgotten," she whispers. "I will fight for your life and for my release."

The vengeful queen forces Albrecht to dance, but as Giselle sways with him, her love tames the frantic music. No longer is Giselle the weak and feverish peasant girl; she now possesses the endurance of a Wili, though her heart has not hardened.

"Please, Myrtha, let Albrecht live," Giselle begs.

"He must dance till he dies," answers the queen.

But the strength of Giselle's love is triumphing over Myrtha's will. It is almost dawn, and Myrtha's power will soon fade. The heartless queen has no intention of waiting any longer.

"He must die! Now, Wilis—kill him!"

The demonic music that signaled Hilarion's fate is heard again. Albrecht is forced to perform the same desperate dance and soon collapses on the ground. Myrtha is about to claim her prize when a bell chimes, heralding the dawn. She covers her eyes as if blinded by light. Giselle's love has outwitted Myrtha, and the queen, now powerless, floats away, surrounded by her Wilis.

Giselle helps Albrecht to his feet and they embrace, knowing that this is goodbye.

Giselle ACT II

Giselle

Giselle returns to her grave. Her spirit is free now and her soul is at peace. Albrecht is left alone in the forest clearing beside the simple tomb. Closing his eyes, he lifts his face to the sky and feels the force of Giselle's love, stronger even than death.

— the curtain falls —

As Giselle sways with Albrecht, her love tames the frantic music.

The Nutcracker

Act I

On a snowy Christmas Eve in Nuremberg, the air is fragrant with the smell of gingerbread and roasting chestnuts. White twists of smoke rise from the chimneys, and colored lights twinkle in every window, while the shimmering Christmas music promises magic to come.

Dr. Stahlbaum's comfortable home is alive with final preparations for the annual Christmas party. The mistletoe must still be hung, and a few last-minute gifts need wrapping. While the grown-ups bustle about, Marie and Fritz, Dr. Stahlbaum's small children, doze in the hallway beside the drawing-room door.

"Wake up, Fritz," says Marie with a yawn. "It's almost time!"

They peer anxiously through the keyhole into the drawing room, trying to catch a glimpse of the Christmas tree.

"Papa's hanging an angel on the tree!" Marie exclaims.

"I can see Mama with an armful of presents!" cries Fritz, jumping up and down.

Soon the Stahlbaums' friends and family begin arriving, dressed in their holiday silks and satins. Little cousins and friends join Marie and Fritz outside the drawing room, each one elated at the thought of the hidden tree.

The music vibrates with excitement, and at the stroke of nine the doors of the drawing room burst open to reveal the magical tree, ablaze with candles and sparkling with colored glass decorations. As the children gaze in awe at the spectacle, Dr. and Mrs. Stahlbaum embrace their guests.

The children soon beg for games, dances, and presents. Dr. Stahlbaum signals for the entertainment to begin, and some of the boys perform an energetic little march. Under the doting eyes of parents and grandparents, aunts and uncles, the girls step onto the floor and, partnered by the boys, dance a formal quadrille.

Some of the parents, carried away by the joyous music, join in the dancing. Refreshments are passed round, and presents are finally exchanged. The little girls are delighted to find lovely china dolls under the tissue and ribbons, while the boys smile with pleasure at their bugles and drums.

Abruptly the music stops. A quizzical melody slowly rises. Everyone's attention is drawn to the old grandfather clock which marks each hour in a very disconcerting fashion: an ugly carved owl, perched on top, beats its wings rhythmically. Just as the owl announces the time, a mysterious dark figure enters the room.

"Who is that?" whispers a nervous Fritz.

"I know," answers Marie.

When the stranger removes his cape and hat, it is obvious to everyone: Herr Drosselmeyer, the creator of the clock, has arrived.

"Godfather!" squeals Marie, her delight, as always, mixed with awe at the sight of this old family friend.

The old man looks startlingly like an owl himself. He is thin and birdlike and dressed all in black, with a patch over one eye and a fine web of wrinkles covering his face. A handsome young boy accompanies him.

"Good evening, friends," says Drosselmeyer. "Marie, come and meet my nephew."

Marie steps forward shyly and blushes when she is introduced to young Drosselmeyer. The new friends soon join the other children, who are staring at three gigantic boxes that Herr Drosselmeyer has brought to the party. The clockmaker wastes no time. He unveils his latest inventions—three life-size dolls. They are Harlequin the clown, his sweetheart, Columbine, and a toy soldier. Drosselmeyer waves his arms like a magician, and the dolls come to life, each performing a mechanical dance.

While the children debate whether the dolls are alive or not, Drosselmeyer beckons to Marie.

"And now a special toy for you, my little Marie."

The Nutcracker ACT I

The old man hands her a funny-looking wooden soldier painted red, blue, and gold. Its head is much too large for its body, and its enormous mouth displays a huge set of teeth.

"This is the Nutcracker," says her godfather.

A wide-eyed Marie takes the toy. She has never seen anything to equal it in the whole world.

"Thank you, Godfather!"

Drosselmeyer shows the children how to crack a nut in the Nutcracker's jaw.

"Gently . . . like this," he explains, and shells a walnut. He returns the toy to Marie, who shows it off to her friends.

Fritz has grown angrier by the minute. "Why is there nothing for me, while my sister gets such a fine toy? Give me that thing!"

He grabs the Nutcracker roughly from Marie, and it smashes to the floor.

"Fritz, how can you be so cruel?" she sobs. "My poor Nutcracker!"

Marie is quickly aided by Drosselmeyer and his gallant nephew. The boy chases Fritz away, while Drosselmeyer bandages the Nutcracker's broken jaw with a handkerchief.

Cradling the wounded Nutcracker, Marie rejoins her girl friends. They rock their dolls to a soothing lullaby, but the peace is soon broken. The boys, banging their drums and blowing their bugles, charge into the little domestic circle.

In the midst of the din, Drosselmeyer's nephew offers Marie a little doll's bed for her injured toy. Marie gratefully puts her Nutcracker to rest under the Christmas tree.

The parents, realizing how tired their children are, join in a final dance to an old folk song. Marie dances with her handsome new friend before the party comes to an end and the guests bid the Stahlbaums goodnight.

"Perhaps we'll meet again soon," suggests young Drosselmeyer.

"I hope so," smiles Marie.

*   *   *

The drawing room is empty and dark. The Stahlbaum household is fast asleep, except for Marie. She longs to see her Nutcracker once more. She tiptoes into

Drosselmeyer bandages the Nutcracker's broken jaw with a handkerchief.

the drawing room in her nightgown and lifts the toy from its bed; but, in the dark, the familiar room seems a strange, mysterious place. Just a little bit afraid, she hugs the Nutcracker close and lies down on the sofa. In spite of her fears, Marie is soon asleep, and the household is quiet again. Or is it?

Someone waits in the shadows—Herr Drosselmeyer. How did he get into the house, and what is he up to? The venerable inventor slips the Nutcracker from Marie's hands, and, as she sleeps, he removes the bandage and mends its broken jaw with a few deft turns of a screwdriver. The old man returns the wooden figure to the sleeping child, but the little girl is not to have a peaceful rest tonight.

Suddenly the Christmas tree blazes with light, and Marie wakes up with a terrible start. Her heart pounds furiously as she surveys the room.

"Godfather!" she cries. "What are you doing here? You frightened me." There is Drosselmeyer, flapping his arms in the owl's place above the clock, but he doesn't answer Marie.

"I had better put you safely away," Marie tells her Nutcracker as she tucks him back into his little bed. And she is just in the nick of time, for at the stroke of twelve an enormous mouse scurries into the drawing room.

"How horrible!" Marie shudders.

Now such terrible rustlings and scratchings shake the room that Marie is certain the house is alive. Music whistles like a high wind, spins through the air, and wraps her in a marvelous melody.

Before her eyes, the Christmas tree begins growing, climbing higher and higher; yet no matter how high it grows, it never seems to reach the ceiling. Perhaps the walls of the room are growing too! The Nutcracker's little bed is life-size now, and the sleeping Nutcracker is bigger than Marie. Even Fritz's toy soldiers, stored in a wooden cabinet, are growing taller by the second.

Marie can't decide whether to be frightened or delighted, when suddenly hordes of huge gray mice, their eyes glinting in the darkness, scamper out of the walls toward her.

"Help!" she screams.

The toy soldiers emerge from the cabinet and mass into formation. A shot is fired, and the battle begins. Trumpets, flutes, and drums urge the struggling soldiers on, but they are a poor match for the ferocious mice. Marie, terrified,

There is Drosselmeyer, flapping his arms in the owl's place above the clock.

wakes the Nutcracker. With the Nutcracker now leading the troops, the brave soldiers fight on, but just as they have managed to take their first mouse prisoner, a horrible creature blackens their path. A hissing, squealing mouse with seven heads, each one wearing a crown, leaps to the front of his troops. He is the Mouse King, and he is so enraged to find one of his mice being dragged along the floor that he orders a fresh attack on the weary soldiers. The Nutcracker, his sword poised, orders the cannon into position, and a round of cheese is fired at the enemy.

Marie can barely make out what is happening on the battlefield for the smoke, clatter, and chaos, but, as the air clears, she sees the huge mice carrying the poor toy soldiers away. Marie stands by helplessly as the Nutcracker is left alone to face the horrible Mouse King's sword. Seeing that her dear Nutcracker is about to be run through by the villain's blade, Marie rips off her slipper and hurls it at the beast. A direct hit! The vicious Mouse King is stunned, and the Nutcracker thrusts his sword through the creature's heart. Victorious, the Nutcracker slices off a golden crown from one of the monster's many heads, and the battle is won.

Marie swoons and falls onto the Nutcracker's bed. As the music gently plays, wonderful, magical things begin to happen. The Christmas tree rises into the air, the French windows mysteriously part, and the bed hovers above the floor like a flying carpet. With the Nutcracker guiding the way, the bed sails into the snowy night.

"I'm not even cold!" Marie whispers to herself. "Where are we going, Nutcracker?"

As the bed lands softly in the snow, the Nutcracker turns to answer her. Now she sees that he is no longer a wooden fellow, but a handsome young prince who looks just like Drosselmeyer's nephew.

"We are on our way to the most delicious place in the world," he smiles, and he hands Marie the crown of the Mouse King.

The falling snowflakes are magically transformed into beautiful maidens, who leap through the air in whirling patterns. A chorus of young, shining voices hums a vibrant tune.

"This is the most wonderful night of my life!" Marie thinks, as she and her prince walk hand in hand into the forest.

The Nutcracker ACT II

Act II

Twelve charming little angels, led by their lovely queen, the Sugar Plum Fairy, await the arrival of Marie and the prince in the delicious Land of Sweets. A lazy lemonade river winds over chocolate hills. A sugar swan settles on the lake, basking in the warmth of a cinnamon sun. Ladyfinger mountain peaks are capped with whipped cream. And everywhere, everything is colored with the most beautiful shades of buttercream frosting.

A delicate melody plays and the Sugar Plum Fairy dances sweetly, her angels gazing at her with love and admiration. At the end of her dance, all the inhabitants of the Land of Sweets assemble to greet Marie and the prince as they navigate their walnut-shell boat into port.

When they disembark, the prince introduces Marie to the Sugar Plum Fairy.

"Have you traveled far? What have you seen?" asks the fairy.

The prince reenacts his perilous adventures, demonstrating how he had been asleep when the mice attacked and how he had risen to lead his troops against them. He finishes with an exciting re-creation of his duel to the death with the Mouse King.

"If it wasn't for Marie's well-aimed slipper, I would have been killed. Her bravery enabled me to deal the final blow to my enemy."

Marie is proud and happy.

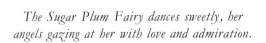

The Sugar Plum Fairy dances sweetly, her angels gazing at her with love and admiration.

The Sugar Plum Fairy, impressed with their noble deeds, escorts them to a candied throne, where a banquet of every imaginable sweet awaits them.

"Bring on the entertainment!" commands the queen.

The dancing is as appetizing as the feast. Hot Chocolates perform a gay Spanish fandango to lilting trumpets. Coffee, a veiled harem girl, weaves her body in sinuous curves to a mysterious song of Arabia. A spicy chorus of flutes introduces the cheerful Mandarin Teas. Marie licks her lips as scores of Candy Canes leap across the stage, performing circus stunts with their hoops. There are Marzipan shepherdesses playing sugar pipes, and finally, to Marie's great amusement, Mother Ginger, as big and wide as a house, waddles across the floor. She parts her voluminous skirts and out charge her little clowns, the polichinelles. Kicking their legs to the happy melody, they dance in a circle around bemused Mother Ginger, then obediently crawl back under her petticoats as she toddles off.

A harp introduces Marie to the loveliest waltz she has ever heard, the Waltz of the Flowers. The radiant flowers dance in weaving patterns as a single dewdrop, flying among them, alights here and there.

And still there is more. A hush falls over the court of the Sugar Plum Fairy. The queen's cavalier, exquisitely handsome, takes her in his arms. She balances regally on his arm, and then he lifts her high in the air. Joyously, the cavalier spins and turns, inspiring the Sugar Plum Fairy to dance for him. To the ethereal sound of a celesta, she steps as delicately as if she were dancing on clouds of spun sugar. When their duet comes to an end and the cavalier holds his queen, Marie thinks, "Now I have seen perfect happiness."

All the inhabitants of the land return to dance an affectionate farewell to the young couple.

"Goodbye! Goodbye!" they chime, as Marie and the prince are led to a sleigh drawn by reindeer. As the sleigh carries them up into the sky, they look back upon the candied world, and Marie turns to her prince and says, "I wish this glorious adventure would never end!"

And it never will, for wonderful things will always be seen by those who have the eyes to see them.

— the curtain falls —

Petrouchka

Scene I

A heavy snow is falling on a cold winter morning in old St. Petersburg. It is the opening of the Shrovetide Fair, a Russian carnival held just before Lent, and a boisterous crowd bundled in coats, colorful scarves, and fur hats mingles in the public square. They ward off the chill by beating their arms against their sides, but their spirits are so warm and glowing that the effort hardly seems necessary. The music quickens and swirls like the wind, pushing the crowd along. On a balcony high above the carnival booths, an old man beckons to passersby. He pats his long white beard proudly and jokes with the crowd. Soldiers flirt with the pretty women, children line up for the merry-go-round, fortune tellers call for customers, and a man lifts a bottle of vodka to his lips, celebrating in his own way.

A brightly dressed young woman rolls out a little piece of carpet on the snow and, striking her triangle, begins to dance. Soon another girl approaches, and to the wistful sounds of an organ grinder, the two display their dancing skills as they vie for the approval of the spectators. When the competition ends, they are rewarded with applause, and the music of the fair resumes. Five bearded peasants in dark traditional dress are inspired to dance by the irresistible melody. They bend low, kicking out their feet from side to side and planting their heels firmly on the pavement. But their dance doesn't hold the arena for long, and once again the fun-loving crowd swarms through the square. The old man on the balcony dangles a fishing pole with a paper fish into this swirling sea of life. Just when it seems as if nothing could capture the attention of the noisy mob, a

Petrouchka SCENE I

loud drum roll startles the crowd into silence. All eyes turn to a stage with a sign that reads "Living Theater."

The Charlatan pokes his head out from behind the bright-blue curtain and surveys the audience. He wears a tall wizard's hat and has a pointed yellow beard and a pale-gray face.

"What is he going to do?" the people wonder.

The Charlatan comes out from behind the curtain, his satin robe trailing through the powdery snow as he slowly raises a flute to his lips. He plays an eerie melody and leaves notes hanging on the cold, clear air like question marks. The crowd scarcely breathes, so hypnotic is the magic tune.

"Bravo, bravo!" they applaud.

The old Charlatan bows low, and then, at a wave of his magic flute, the curtains part to reveal his creations—three life-size puppets: Petrouchka the clown on the right, the Moor on the left, and in the center, the Ballerina. They wait in separate alcoves, each puppet supported on a stand equipped with armrests to hold their bodies in place as their legs dangle down.

Again the Charlatan waves his flute, and, one by one, he brings his puppets to life. They move like mechanical toys, dancing furiously to the unrelenting music. Occasionally they bend their knees and lift them up to their chests, but for the most part their feet simply brush the floor beneath them. At a signal from the puppeteer, they fly off their stands and scamper into the square, their movements so quick and complicated they have a dizzying effect.

"Wonderful!" the crowd marvels. "They seem almost alive."

The Ballerina blows kisses in the air while she dances pertly on her toes. She has a doll-like porcelain face with bright-red lips, circles of rouge on her cheeks, and long painted eyelashes. Her crinoline bounces as she performs her intricate steps without visible effort. The Moor too dances with authority, his white eyes and teeth gleaming in his coal-black face. Perfumes of exotic lands seem to rise from his silk costume. Only the clown Petrouchka appears out of control. Although he dances at high speed, he looks reluctant; he wishes the Charlatan would let him rest. His head flops against his shoulder, and his back bends as if there weren't enough straw stuffed in his clothes to keep him upright. His sorrowful face is painted chalky white, but, unlike the others, he seems to have real flesh beneath.

Both the Moor and Petrouchka are in love with the Ballerina. Petrouchka edges toward the porcelain doll, but she is confused by the clown's attentions and moves closer to the Moor. Observing all this carefully, the Charlatan calls Petrouchka to him, places a club under his arm, and sends him back. As the Ballerina huddles in the Moor's arms, Petrouchka attacks his rival with the club in a fit of jealousy. But Petrouchka is no match for the much larger Moor. In a panic, the clown drops the club and tries to run away, but he stumbles and falls. The Moor triumphantly straddles the little puppet.

On the Charlatan's command, Petrouchka rises and the three resume their performance as if nothing had happened. They finish their dance and take a bow along with the Charlatan. The music stops abruptly and, with an ominous drum roll, the curtain falls on the Shrovetide Fair.

Scene II

Bright white stars cover the inky-black walls of a simple cell. Clouds decorate the ceiling and icy mountain peaks crowd the baseboard. On one wall, a portrait of the Charlatan looms menacingly. It is the dark, despairing interior of Petrouchka's room in the Living Theater.

The door opens and a violent kick from the Charlatan sends Petrouchka sliding across the floor on his stomach. The door slams shut. The clown lies motionless, then his body jerks spasmodically as if he were reluctantly returning to life. With great effort, poor Petrouchka rises to his knees, and then, remembering his awful life, throws his arms to the heavens and collapses again.

"I must find a way out," he thinks, and like a caged animal the desperate clown frantically circles the room, banging his straw hands against the walls. In the background, Petrouchka's melody, urgent and questioning, plays. The music erupts with a piercing cry as he stretches his stiff arms toward his master's picture.

"Why have you created me, a doll of straw in a cold, silent world?"

He pounds his chest and reaches out for an answer from his master's image, but no answer comes. "No," Petrouchka gestures. "I am real, and I have a heart that aches to prove it."

The music grows softer and calms the distraught puppet. He rubs his clumsy hands against his painted cheek. Slowly, he remembers the Ballerina and he blows a kiss at the door, wishing she were with him.

"But what's the use?" he thinks to himself. "She doesn't care," and he pounds his head with his hands to punish himself.

Suddenly the door opens.

"Go, my Ballerina, go to Petrouchka," coaxes the Charlatan.

He slams the door quickly, and the wide-eyed dancer steps forward stiffly on her toes. She bends over at the waist and greets the clown.

"She's come!" Petrouchka thinks with delight, but his awkward enthusiasm scares the shy Ballerina, and she rushes from his cell.

The door opens magically for her, but when Petrouchka tries to follow her, it locks. Defeated, he backs into a corner and cowers like a frightened dog.

"Yes," he nods, "this is the way it always is."

Then, in one last desperate burst of energy, Petrouchka rushes around the room, banging on all the walls, both high and low.

"I have a heart!" he shrieks at the portrait. "Release me!"

The little clown lunges angrily at the painting. To his shock, the wall rips open like a tear in the universe and he falls forward. He hangs there suspended, half in, half out of the cell. Then, frightened, he rears back into his room, and gazes with awe at the hole.

Overwhelmed by the powers that control him, Petrouchka begs the Charlatan's portrait for mercy and collapses, his straw arms stretched out at his sides, his puppet's body pressed flat against the hard floor.

Scene III

Unlike Petrouchka's dark and gloomy cell, the Moor's room glows with the warmth of a painted tropical sun. The Moor lies in comfort on his cushioned chaise, surrounded by brilliantly colored walls of jungle palms. He passes the time by tossing a coconut in the air to the lazy rhythm of an exotic melody. When he has had enough of the couch, he somersaults to the floor and shakes his precious coconut next to his ear to discover its secrets. He tries to take a bite out of it, but its hard shell resists his teeth. In a fit of childish rage, he thrashes the coconut with his scimitar, but it still doesn't crack.

Petrouchka SCENE II

"If it won't open, it must be a powerful god," he reasons, and bows low before the coconut.

The sound of a trumpet interrupts his meditation, and the Charlatan sends in the pretty Ballerina. Surprised by the intrusion, the Moor covers the coconut with his body and watches the Ballerina as she hops mechanically around the room on pointed toes, playing on her horn. Gradually her dance draws the Moor to her. He holds the Ballerina roughly by the waist as she leans against him, his big feet plodding along. She seems to enjoy his clumsy efforts and allows him to spin her around, her leg raised high and her arms poised above her head.

The Moor then sits on the floor and applauds delightedly as the Ballerina resumes her solo dance. After a few turns, she falls sideways into his lap. Pleased, he begins nibbling on her like a piece of fruit. Although surprised, the Ballerina enjoys his attentions and stays put.

"This is very nice," the brutish Moor thinks.

They dance together once again, but this time he puts his hands around her waist and pulls her toward the couch. Though pretending to be shocked, the Ballerina follows him and lands contentedly in his lap on the soft cushions.

The muffled sound of Petrouchka's melody is heard, and the little clown appears in the doorway. The amorous couple jump up from the couch, and Petrouchka, imagining the Ballerina needs protection from the Moor's advances, rushes into the room. But the Moor resents this invasion of his private lair and chases Petrouchka round and round while the anxious Ballerina follows closely on their heels. Finally, Petrouchka's soft body weakens and he falls to the ground. The raging giant picks up the humiliated clown by the waist, spins him around heartlessly, and kicks him squarely out through the door.

The Ballerina and her paramour return to the couch and sit, just as before, in empty-headed bliss.

Scene IV

At twilight, the revelers are still celebrating in the public square. The merry-go-round spins to the same swirling melody that played in the morning, and people drink hot tea from samovars to brace themselves in the chilly evening air. When the music changes to an exhilarating folk song, a group of nursemaids, handkerchiefs flying, zigzag about the fairground. So irresistible are the tune and the movement that a band of coachmen dance along too.

The music stops abruptly when a big brown bear lumbers through the crowd. The bear's trainer is not far behind, and as he passes round a tin money cup, he laughs at the fear of the onlookers.

The nursemaids pull ribbons from a vendor's cart, and gypsy fortune tellers dance on either arm of an elegant gentleman. The coachmen take the floor and, crouching low, do a vigorous dance on their heels. As they bounce up and down, their arms trace huge circles in the air. They are rejoined by the nursemaids, whose billowing skirts catch the falling snow as they twirl joyfully.

A piercing cry rings out, and a sudden movement from behind the Charlatan's blue curtain draws the crowd's attention. To the amazement of the merrymakers, the puppets come running out of the Living Theater, but this time the Charlatan isn't pulling the strings. Petrouchka is being chased by the Moor, and the Ballerina, in panic, is close behind. With a single, terrible blow of his scimitar, the Moor fells the cornered Petrouchka, and the clown collapses on the wet pavement.

Everyone forms a respectful circle around the body and waits. Out of the long silence, quivering music from the strings is heard. The little clown's body jerks convulsively, as if fighting for life. He lifts his head and stretches his arm toward the wondering throng. He seems to ask, "Why do I suffer? Could I be human too?" He pauses a moment, as if waiting for an answer, but his strength gives way and he sinks senseless to the ground.

"He's dead!" the crowd exclaims. "Find a policeman!"

After examining the body, an officer searches the square and finds the Charlatan among the spectators. He stops him for questioning.

"What has happened here? Are you responsible for this murder, old man?"

"That pile of cloth was not alive. How could it be killed?" the Charlatan answers, and he lifts the clown by the scruff of the neck. Sure enough, it is a limp doll of straw, nothing more.

The witnesses, though astonished, accept what their eyes now tell them. They turn their backs on the puppeteer and his creation and slowly make their way home.

Petrouchka

The Charlatan is dragging the stuffed doll toward the theater when he hears the faint cry of a horn—Petrouchka's cry. The wizard looks up and sees Petrouchka's ghost on the roof of the theater, laughing into the night, mocking his disbelieving master. The Charlatan drops the straw puppet in terror and runs from the fairground. Petrouchka raises his arms to the heavens, then abruptly falls forward, his body dangling lifelessly over the marquee, his soul finally free.

— the curtain falls —

Petrouchka raises his arms to the heavens, then abruptly falls forward, his body dangling lifelessly.

Petrouchka SCENE III

Romeo and Juliet

Act I

SCENE I

Early-morning light floods the empty marketplace in old Verona. Young Romeo, the son of Lord Montague, enters the square in pursuit of Rosaline, a member of the house of Capulet. When she ignores his advances, Romeo is not surprised—the Capulets and the Montagues have been feuding for years. But Romeo bears no ill will toward the Capulets.

Benvolio and Mercutio, two of Romeo's friends, join him in the marketplace. As the shopkeepers and their patrons begin to arrive, the square comes alive with activity and music.

Three village girls saunter boldly toward Romeo and his friends and invite them to dance. In the midst of the dancing, the Capulet Tybalt and a band of his kinsmen approach, brandishing swords.

"Draw your sword, vile Montague!" Tybalt cries out to Romeo.

"I have no quarrel with you," Romeo answers gaily.

"When you mock our family by flirting with Rosaline, you beg for a fight."

As the music storms, Mercutio leaps to meet Tybalt's challenge. Before long, the marketplace is filled with battling Capulets and Montagues.

Alerted by the sounds of battle, the Prince of Verona enters the square to find nearly a dozen men lying dead on the stones.

"Enough!" he cries. "This fighting will stop!"

The prince commands his subjects to carry the dead to the center of the square. Pointing to the carnage, he proclaims, "There will be no more bloodshed. I demand peace in my domain."

Romeo is the first to respond, laying down his sword before the bodies. Against their will, the warring Montagues and Capulets follow suit.

SCENE 2

Juliet, the daughter of Lord Capulet, enters her bedroom. Her old nurse watches with delight as Juliet tosses a doll in the air to a lovely melody. Though Juliet is approaching womanhood, she is still in many ways a child.

Her parents, accompanied by Paris, Juliet's fiancé, enter the chamber. Paris kisses the young girl's hand with obvious pleasure, but Juliet dances out of his reach.

"Never mind, Paris. She'll soon grow up and make you a good wife," Lord Capulet apologizes.

Paris bows graciously and departs, and Lord and Lady Capulet follow. Juliet rushes back to her doll, but this time her nurse discourages the game.

"Give me the doll, dear. You're no longer a child—you'll be married soon."

Juliet blushes in bewilderment.

SCENE 3

Outside the iron gates of Lord Capulet's villa, Romeo, Benvolio, and Mercutio, disguised in masks, watch the guests arriving for a party. Romeo, protected by his disguise, flirts openly with Rosaline before she passes through the gate on Tybalt's arm.

"She isn't so beautiful," Benvolio teases Romeo. "I'll bet there are dozens of pretty girls inside. Why don't we go in and find out?"

The music, mimicking the boys' high spirits, is ripe with mischief. They dance, kicking their legs like young stallions, and merrily pass through the iron gates into the house of Lord Capulet.

SCENE 4

A courtly dance is under way when Romeo and his friends enter the ballroom. Juliet, brimming with excitement, descends the staircase and is met by the gallant Paris. With Lady Capulet's approval, Paris invites Juliet to dance. Her innocent beauty sets her apart from the other girls, and as Romeo stares in amazement, wondering who she is, Juliet turns from Paris and sees Romeo. Their eyes meet and their love is born.

Juliet's girl friends ask her to play the mandolin for them while they dance. Romeo, unable to restrain himself, approaches Juliet. The shy maidens flee, and Romeo, inspired by his love, dances for Juliet. At the conclusion of his dance, the young man kneels at her feet and gently takes the mandolin from her hands.

*Her old nurse watches in delight as Juliet tosses
a doll in the air.*

Romeo and Juliet ACT I, Scene 4

Paris rushes jealously to Juliet's side, but she ignores him, and while Romeo strums the mandolin, she dances for his eyes alone.

"Romeo, don't you know who this girl is? We must leave at once!" plead Benvolio and Mercutio.

But it is too late for warnings. Taking Juliet by the waist, Romeo spins her in his arms.

The loyal Mercutio, fearful for his Montague friend in this alien Capulet house, dances wildly to distract attention from the couple. His plan succeeds temporarily, although Tybalt, the most hostile of the Capulets, watches Mercutio's mocking performance with suspicion.

The guests tire of dancing, and everyone leaves the ballroom. Juliet returns alone. Romeo finds her and removes his mask. Drawn together, they dance with an affection and contentment that neither has known before.

Tybalt, suspicious of the three masked partygoers, stalks back into the hall. To threatening music, he approaches the couple and recognizes Romeo.

"Get away from my cousin Juliet!" he cries, and shoves Romeo.

Lord Capulet returns to witness the confrontation.

"I don't want to fight you," declares Romeo. "Take my hand, good Tybalt."

Tybalt is only further enraged and pushes Romeo again and again.

"This lad, Montague or not, is a guest in my home. Let him be," intercedes Lord Capulet.

The curious guests have gathered around the quarreling pair. In a gesture of friendship, a Capulet lady takes Romeo's hand and urges him to partner her. Others join in the dancing, and peace is restored to the ballroom. Romeo, however, finds his way back to Juliet, and as the two dance, Tybalt can scarcely suppress his anger.

Mercutio is surprised at Romeo's total lack of good sense. When the ball ends, Benvolio and Mercutio usher their stubborn friend away.

SCENE 5

Juliet is standing on her balcony in the moonlight, wishing her new love were beside her, when Romeo enters the garden below. Delighted that her secret prayers have been answered, Juliet descends the stairs into the garden.

Romeo is unable to restrain his joy at seeing Juliet, and leaps high in the air, spinning deliriously. With this declaration of love, Juliet falls into his arms and they dance. Overcome with happiness, Romeo kneels before her and kisses the hem of her skirt. She leans against his strong arms as he rocks her gently to the romantic music.

Their time together passes quickly. The dawn is breaking and they must part.

"Goodnight, my love," Juliet whispers, as she mounts the stairs to her balcony and disappears inside.

Act II

SCENE I

Romeo wanders through the busy marketplace, oblivious to the antics of the crowd. Indignant wives berate their husbands, who flirt audaciously with the village lasses. Romeo is accosted by the brazen girls, but he motions them away. When the good-humored Benvolio and Mercutio enter the marketplace, they are more receptive to the amorous advances.

"If Romeo is too distracted to dance with a pretty girl, he must be in love," they agree.

Romeo overhears his friends and he smiles. Happy to be alive, he dances the breadth of the square. When he spies a wedding procession entering the marketplace, he insists on kissing the bride.

"One day that will be Juliet and I," he thinks.

As he dances with the young bride, Juliet's trusted nurse enters. The merriment has infected the three friends, and Benvolio, Mercutio, and Romeo tease her mercilessly.

"Now if you'll stop teasing and tell me which one of you is Romeo, I have a note here from my little mistress."

Romeo kisses her in delight and takes the letter.

"Dear Romeo," he reads. "I too wish with all my heart to be married at once."

A joyful Romeo gives the old nurse another kiss and hurries away.

SCENE 2

Soft music floats through Friar Laurence's stone cell while the friar bows his head in prayer.

Romeo enters the little chapel. "Friar Laurence, please read this letter. Juliet has consented to marry me, and I beg you to perform the ceremony."

"But, my son, how can I when your families would forbid it?"

At that moment, the nurse enters, followed by Juliet. When Friar Laurence sees Romeo and Juliet together, he is forced to change his mind.

"Perhaps their love will reunite their families in peace," he thinks.

Romeo and Juliet join hands and kneel before the friar, and he pronounces them man and wife. The good nurse weeps and then, reluctantly separating the couple, wraps Juliet in her cloak and takes her home.

SCENE 3

Benvolio and Mercutio are still dancing in the marketplace. Mercutio is joking in his usual fashion. The Capulet Tybalt looks on disdainfully, and with every gulp of wine he takes, he grows angrier with Romeo's friend. Violent music foretells disaster as Tybalt threatens Mercutio with his sword. Undaunted, Mercutio unsheathes his own blade and they begin fighting.

Romeo, the real target of Tybalt's rage, enters the square.

"Draw your sword, coward!" Tybalt challenges Romeo.

But Romeo does not want to fight with his new kinsman.

"Tybalt, let's forget our quarrel. Mercutio, put down your sword."

Mercutio, unaware that Tybalt is now Romeo's cousin, thinks Romeo is afraid. Determined to defend his friend, he continues to fight. He lunges merrily at Tybalt and knocks the weapon from his hand. Tybalt stares in dread at his enemy, expecting death; but Mercutio, happy to end the duel without bloodshed, returns the sword to Tybalt and walks away. Tybalt treacherously stabs the good Mercutio in the back.

Romeo's dearest friend is dead. "I'll have vengeance!" he shouts at Tybalt.

The crowd braces for more killing as a desperate battle ensues. This time a Montague is victorious as Romeo's sword sinks into Tybalt's heart.

*"Tybalt, let's forget our quarrel. Mercutio, put
down your sword."*

Lady Capulet enters the square to find Tybalt lying dead.

"Forgive me," Romeo begs.

But Lady Capulet is deaf to his pleas. "Murderer!" she wails, cradling her dead nephew in her arms.

Act III

SCENE I

Juliet lies in Romeo's embrace on her canopied bed. The sun is rising. Romeo gets up, wraps himself in his cloak, and walks toward the balcony.

"It's time for me to leave," he says sadly.

"But the prince has banished you from Verona, and I don't know when we'll meet again. Please stay!"

"If I stay any longer, they'll throw me into prison."

The music grieves with them. They dance together, and as the time ticks away, their dance grows more tortured. Again and again, Juliet falls into Romeo's arms. She holds tightly onto his legs, then his waist, trying desperately to restrain him, to keep him with her one more moment.

"Goodbye, my darling. I'll never stop loving you." Romeo kisses her for the last time and flees from the room.

Juliet can think of nothing but Romeo. When her mother and father enter with Paris, Juliet turns from him in disgust.

"How can you be so rude, Juliet? After all, you're going to marry Paris very soon," her mother scolds.

"Please, mother! Don't make me marry him," she sobs violently.

Angered by her behavior, Lord Montague strikes his daughter. Realizing that protest is useless, Juliet finally calms herself and dances to a tragic melody before falling exhausted to the floor. Her angry parents, followed by Paris, leave the room.

"What can I do?" she weeps. "I must ask Friar Laurence."

She puts on her cloak and hurries to the monk's cell.

SCENE 2

Juliet kneels before Friar Laurence and begs him for help.

"It's impossible for you to tell your parents you are married to Romeo. We must find another way. Are you courageous enough to follow my instructions?"

"I'd sooner die than marry Paris."

Friar Laurence hands her a small phial of liquid. "Drink this sleeping potion. You'll appear to be dead, but you'll only be asleep. After your body is taken to the family crypt, I'll contact Romeo and explain to him what I've done. He'll take you away from Verona, and after enough time has passed, I'll tell your parents that you're alive and married to a Montague."

Juliet is frightened, but she sees no other solution. Friar Laurence blesses her, and, firmly resolved to drink the potion, Juliet leaves for home.

SCENE 3

Juliet is gazing out of the window of her room when she hears footsteps approaching. She hides the sleeping potion under her pillow and turns to find her nurse, her parents, and her fiancé at the door.

Juliet begs one last time to be released from marriage to Paris, but her father angrily insists that she go through with it. She pretends to give in to her father's command and agrees to dance with Paris. The music is full of mystery and tinged with doom.

But Juliet cannot hide her feelings for long. She pushes Paris away and runs to the window. Poor Paris kisses her skirt, trying to prove his genuine affection, but Juliet is unmoved.

"Juliet, you'll marry Paris, and that is my final word," orders Lord Capulet, turning from the room. Lady Capulet, Paris, and the nurse follow him out.

Juliet grasps the phial and, with grave doubts, drinks the potion. Clutching her stomach in pain, she falls to the floor. Slowly she drags herself to the bed and collapses.

The next morning, six bridesmaids dance into the room, bearing garlands of flowers. "Wake up! It's time for the wedding," they call.

One of them tries to rouse Juliet. "She won't move," the girl whispers. They all back away in fear.

The nurse, carrying Juliet's wedding dress into the room, tries to lift the sleeping girl from her pillow, but Juliet falls back on the bed like a rag doll. The old nurse's screams soon bring Lord and Lady Capulet running.

SCENE 4

Friar Laurence's plan is going all wrong. Romeo has received news of Juliet's death, and he leaves for Verona before the friar's message can reach him. Thinking Juliet truly dead, Romeo procures poison for himself.

Inside the ancient tomb of the Capulets, Juliet is laid out on a stone bier. Her family grieves while robed monks carry candles into the tomb. After their prayers, Lord and Lady Capulet follow the monks out. Paris stays behind to say a last goodbye to Juliet.

One monk lingers in the shadows, watching Paris. It is Romeo in disguise. "I can't bear to see him touch her," Romeo thinks. "If it weren't for him, she'd still be alive." In his pain and confusion, Romeo stabs Paris and kills him.

Romeo cannot believe that Juliet is really dead. He tries to place her arms around his neck, but they fall away. He lifts her in an embrace, but her body slumps back heavily in his arms. He tries to dance with her once again, but she slides from his grasp. In agony, he drags her lifeless form along the ground.

Finally convinced that she is dead, he returns her body to the bier. He takes the poison from his belt and drinks it. "At least we can be together in death."

He hugs his wife and then falls dead.

A bright melody is heard in sharp contrast to this scene of death. Juliet awakes from her long sleep and is frightened by the unfamiliar surroundings. As her eyes search the darkness, she sees two bodies lying on the ground. She soon realizes that one of them is Romeo's.

"My love, you've come for me." Thinking he is only sleeping, she kisses him tenderly. "Your lips are cold! No, it can't be!"

Discovering the bloody dagger, Juliet holds it up for a moment, then plunges it into her breast. Her love for Romeo gives her the final strength she needs. She crawls back to her bier, lifts Romeo's hand, and pulls him toward her. Juliet kisses her own hand, places it tenderly to her husband's cheek, and, with her head nestled against his, dies.

— the curtain falls —

Romeo and Juliet ACT III, Scene 4

The Sleeping Beauty

Prologue

The members of the court of King Florestan XXIV are gathering in the great hall of his palace to celebrate a momentous event. After many years of marriage, the queen has at last borne her first child, and today is Princess Aurora's christening.

The royal master of ceremonies, foolish old Cattalabutte, announces the king and queen. To the sound of trumpets, the proud parents descend the great staircase. The queen gazes tenderly at Aurora, nestled in her silk-lined cradle, while the king confers with Cattalabutte.

"Have you checked the guest list carefully?" he asks.

"Yes, Sire. Over and over again."

"And you're sure you've omitted no one?"

The old man scans the list nervously. "Everything seems to be in order."

A magical melody echoes through the stone hall as Princess Aurora's six fairy godmothers and their escorts arrive, bearing splendid gifts. They bow to the king and queen before dancing a courtly waltz in honor of the royal couple. The fairies then gather round the child to offer their blessings, and one at a time they dance for the little princess. The Fairy of the Crystal Fountain dances demurely, followed by the Fairy of the Enchanted Garden, who spins cheerfully around the room, and the Fairy of the Woodland Glade, who glides regally across the floor. Quick as a hummingbird, the Fairy of the Songbirds flutters her arms to the sound of flutes, and then the Fairy of the Golden Vine dances to a sprightly tune. The beautiful Lilac Fairy is the last to bless Aurora, and her elegant solo is the grandest of all.

The time has come for the fairies to bestow their gifts, and the king and queen step forward to receive them. The Lilac Fairy is the last to offer her present, but before she has a chance to do so, a distant rumble is heard. It rapidly grows louder, until it bursts into a deafening thunder. The king, sensing that this is no ordinary storm, summons Cattalabutte and demands to see the guest list. As he scans the names, his worst fears are confirmed.

"You fool!" he screams at Cattalabutte. "You've forgotten to invite Carabosse."

The hall darkens, and a band of rats creep into the room to the strains of an ominous melody. They are the horrible attendants of Carabosse, the oldest fairy in the kingdom. Once, she too was a beautiful fairy, but her face is now lined with age and anger. Descending from her black carriage, she demands:

"Why wasn't I invited to this christening?"

"But when Aurora reaches her sixteenth birthday, she will prick her finger on this golden spindle and die!"

The king explains that it was an unforgivable oversight on the part of his incompetent master of ceremonies and offers his apologies. Cattalabutte cowers on the floor, and, to torment the old fool, Carabosse tears off his wig and tosses it to the greedy rats. She then addresses the king.

"Your apologies are worthless. But just the same, I have a gift for your child."

The threatening music grows louder. Grasping a golden spindle with her long, pointed fingernails, Carabosse lets loose her terrible curse.

"Your daughter will grow to be a beautiful young woman, the most beautiful in the land. But when she reaches her sixteenth birthday, she will prick her finger on this golden spindle and die!"

The king, in horror, begs her to take back the curse, but it's no use. Carabosse simply laughs at him while the rats grovel at her feet.

The queen sobs uncontrollably at her baby's wretched fate, and the Lilac Fairy tries to comfort her.

"Remember, I haven't given the princess my gift yet. Though it is not in my power to undo the curse of Carabosse, I can soften it. The Princess Aurora will indeed prick her finger on a golden spindle, but instead of dying, she will fall into a deep sleep lasting one hundred years. Everyone in the kingdom will sleep as well, until a handsome prince finds the enchanted castle. He will kiss our beautiful Aurora, restoring her and the court to life."

Carabosse is enraged. "So you think you can trick me. We'll see about that!"

She commands the rats to carry her coach away, leaving behind a puff of smoke as a reminder of her wicked spell.

The grateful king and queen thank the Lilac Fairy, and the music becomes joyful again. The guests all bow to the little princess, while her fairy godmothers hover protectively around her cradle.

Act I

People from all over the kingdom are arriving at the palace to celebrate Princess Aurora's sixteenth birthday. Richly dressed courtiers wander about the palace garden, while, in their midst, three old hags sit hunched over their spinning wheels. This is such an unusual event that many gather round to watch.

The Sleeping Beauty ACT I

Spinning wheels have been outlawed in the kingdom ever since the wicked Carabosse issued her curse sixteen years ago.

Cattalabutte, checking to see that all is in order, spies the wizened hags, seizes their spindles, and orders them to leave the grounds at once. As they tremble before him, the king and queen approach.

"Who are these old women?" the king asks his master of ceremonies. "And what are you holding in your hand?"

To the horror of the king and queen, Cattalabutte reveals the spindles.

"Hang them at once!" the king commands.

But the queen is moved by the entreaties of the frightened old crones.

"Please spare them, dear. They're old, and they may never have read the proclamation. Besides, we don't want anything to spoil the birthday festivities."

The king relents, and the three hags are sent away unharmed.

The festivities begin when the village girls arrive, carrying garlands of flowers high above their heads. They waltz to a rapturous melody, swinging the flower hoops to and fro.

Everyone has been eagerly awaiting the arrival of the princess, and no sooner does Cattalabutte announce her than Aurora rushes down the steps to the garden and embraces her parents.

The king introduces her to four princes, suitors from foreign lands who have come to pay their respects to the king and to meet his beautiful daughter. One by one, they kneel before the princess as she poses in arabesque. Each prince presents her with a single rose, and she delightedly accepts the tributes. She now offers the waiting princes her hand, and each in turn spins her slowly as she poses regally on one toe, her other leg held high behind. Aurora's grace and poise charm them completely. When the dance ends, Aurora runs from the garden, and the young princes look longingly after her.

Eight of the princess's girl friends, in groups of four, link arms and dance as the orchestra plays gaily. Aurora returns to the garden, first dancing sweetly to the delicate strains of a violin, then finishing in bold spins around the floor. The court watches appreciatively as the eight girls resume their waltz, again followed by a glowing Aurora.

The king and his attendants, engrossed in the dance, have failed to notice an uninvited guest, cloaked in black, standing at the back of the garden. The stranger turns toward Aurora and holds out a gleaming object. Assuming it to be a birthday gift, the princess takes it and continues to dance.

"What a lovely toy!" she thinks.

The king catches sight of the object. "The spindle!" he cries in horror. He runs to her side, but it's too late: Aurora has already pricked her finger.

"Father, I feel faint." She revives a little and attempts to finish her dance, but with every step she grows weaker and the music becomes more threatening. As Aurora falls helplessly to the ground, the mysterious figure looms over her. She drops her black cape and reveals herself: it is Carabosse.

Aurora, her eyes closed, lies perfectly still. The wicked fairy laughs as the skies blacken and rain pours down on the grieving kingdom, and then, her terrible vengeance taken, she disappears from the garden in a puff of smoke.

The king and queen think their dear child is dead, but the Lilac Fairy is nearby and comforts them.

"Remember, I modified Carabosse's curse sixteen years ago. Aurora is not dead—she is only asleep. And she will sleep peacefully for one hundred years, until she is awakened by a handsome prince."

The Lilac Fairy directs the four princes to carry Aurora to her chamber, and, as the stricken court follows behind, the good fairy weaves her spell. Everyone in Florestan's kingdom is overcome with sleep: nobles, peasants, servants, soldiers, even the animals. Waving her arms, the Lilac Fairy conjures up a maze of tangled vines which surrounds the palace and its grounds, leaving Carabosse outside to bemoan her thwarted curse.

Act II

SCENE I

One hundred years have passed. At the far reaches of King Florestan's land, a royal hunting party gathers beside a forest lake. Prince Florimund, at the center of the group, offers a toast as his guests drink wine from pewter cups. The prince possesses all the riches and good fortune a man could want, but he is deeply unhappy. One of his companions, a beautiful countess, sees that the prince is not enjoying himself, and she suggests a dance. Reluctantly, Florimund joins the party in a courtly mazurka, but this fails to entertain him for long. Soon the horns signal the hunt, but Prince Florimund urges his companions to proceed without him and remains behind.

The sun sets, the moon rises. Alone in the forest, the prince paces the ground and then dances to a sad melody. He longs for love.

Gazing at the quiet lake, he hears celestial music and sees a silvery boat gliding across the water. The mysterious ship reaches land, and the Lilac Fairy steps ashore.

Prince Florimund bows to his unknown visitor. "Who are you? Why are you here?" he asks.

"I am the Lilac Fairy from the kingdom of King Florestan. The love you've been searching for lives in his palace."

"Who is she?"

"She is the fairest creature in all the land," and the Lilac Fairy tells the prince the story of Aurora and her curse. "You are the one who can wake her with a kiss."

The prince begs to see the Sleeping Beauty, and her image appears, reflected magically on the bark of an oak tree. Florimund, enraptured by her beauty, is crestfallen when the vision vanishes, but he is soon cheered when it reappears in another place, this time surrounded by fairies. Princess Aurora, as real as life, dances toward Florimund, and he lifts her high above the forest floor to slow and tender music. Aurora rejoins the fairies and dances in their midst. Florimund tries to touch her but is restrained by the Lilac Fairy. Finally, the princess approaches him. Resting her arm on his shoulder, she balances on one foot, allowing him to turn her gently. Then, rushing from the prince, she once again steps into the circle formed by the fairies. The prince chases her through this maze, his heart bursting with love.

When at last he catches her, the sad melody swells with hope. "I wish to marry Aurora," he tells the Lilac Fairy.

With this declaration, the melancholy music turns joyful as all the fairies dance in celebration. Florimund and Aurora share one last moment together before the image of Aurora vanishes abruptly.

The prince is heartbroken.

The Sleeping Beauty ACT II, Scene 2

"She was only a vision," the Lilac Fairy reminds him. "Follow me, and we'll sail to the real Aurora's side."

Bathed in mist, the ship bearing the fairy and Florimund sets out across the lake.

SCENE 2

Prince Florimund and the Lilac Fairy step from the magical boat onto a distant shore and, after passing through a dark tunnel of trees, arrive at the gate of King Florestan's castle. Carabosse and her rats have been spying on them from the shadows and run ahead to the palace. Like a ravenous spider, Carabosse peers at the slumbering court through the enormous web that spans the open door.

"Your curse has expired—and so has your power over this kingdom. Now leave us in peace," commands the Lilac Fairy.

Blinded by the fairy's goodness, Carabosse averts her eyes and backs away.

Entering the palace, Florimund is astounded at the sight of hundreds of sleeping people, dressed in old-fashioned clothes and covered with a century of dust.

"But where is the princess?" he whispers to the Lilac Fairy.

The good fairy leads him to Aurora's chamber and points her wand at a canopied bed. There, beneath the cobwebs, lies the Sleeping Beauty, still as young and lovely as the day she fell asleep.

Florimund approaches the princess and kisses her tenderly, and Aurora awakens to find the handsome prince kneeling before her. Slowly, the king and queen rise from their long slumber and greet their savior, Prince Florimund. Cattalabutte wakes up, yawns absentmindedly, and straightens his dusty wig, as one by one all the inhabitants of the kingdom come to life.

"I wish to marry your daughter, Sire," Florimund announces.

"Nothing would please me more," the king responds.

The radiant Aurora dances with her prince, and, to the sound of violins, he takes her in his arms and carries her away.

Act III

It is Aurora's wedding day, and Cattalabutte—still master of ceremonies—pompously enters the great hall. He summons the guests forward, and they promenade to a majestic polonaise. A number of very special guests from fairyland have been invited to this important celebration: Puss in Boots and the White Cat, the Bluebird and the Enchanted Princess, Little Red Riding Hood and the Wolf, and Beauty with her Beast. Of course, the Lilac Fairy is present too, with all her sister fairies.

Every person in the kingdom is at the wedding, and all of them look as fresh as if they had wakened from only one good night's sleep. When the king and queen descend the staircase and assume their thrones, the entertainment begins.

Aurora's younger brother and her two sisters bow before the court. The three link arms and waltz to a sweet melody, expressing their pleasure at Aurora's happiness.

As they return to their seats, the White Cat runs forward, followed by Puss in Boots. Puss tries to pet the cat, but she moves away, peering at him flirtatiously. Even though she occasionally scratches and meows, she really seems to enjoy Puss's attentions, and finally allows him to carry her off the dance floor.

A simple tune announces the Bluebird and his Enchanted Princess. He lifts her high in the air and she poses in flight. Then the Bluebird soars through the sky, his body arching as he jumps, his arms extended high over his head, while the court applauds his daring.

At last, the bride and bridegroom arrive at the celebration. They dance a romantic duet to a melody as fresh and bright as their future. The prince moves with great power and skill, Aurora with grace and charm. Spinning toward him, she dives fearlessly into his arms, as if no danger could ever touch her again. Florimund catches her, and the two pose for the approving crowd.

Now the fairy-tale characters and all the other guests dance a joyous mazurka, led by Aurora and Florimund. When the dance is over, the Lilac Fairy and her attendants surround the happy couple, as the Sleeping Beauty is embraced by the prince who brought her back to life.

— the curtain falls —

Puss in Boots tries to pet the White Cat, but she moves away, peering at him flirtatiously.

Swan Lake

Act I

In a luxurious garden lined with tall oak trees and sweet-scented flowers, picnic tables are covered with food and drink. The brilliant sun chases the shadows from every corner. Why then does the festive music have an air of doom about it?

Peasants and royalty alike are dancing about the garden in celebration of Prince Siegfried's twenty-first birthday. His old tutor, Wolfgang, and his best friend, Benno, lift their glasses to toast the prince as he arrives. Siegfried, a spirited young man with a noble manner, greets them warmly.

"Thank you all for joining me. Shall we drink some wine? Dear Wolfgang, I see you've started already," laughs the prince.

"You know I never refuse a glass, my boy," Wolfgang confesses, and rocks gaily on his feet.

"This is an afternoon made for drink and song," Siegfried replies. "Please, everyone, continue dancing."

A boy and two pretty girls lead the celebration and dance to the light, cheerful music. Their animated performance adds to the festive mood, but the unexpected entrance of the queen mother brings the merriment to a halt.

The guests quiet down and bow to their queen.

Turning to Siegfried, she says, "This is a very serious and important day. Frivolous behavior has no place here." She casts a highly disapproving glance at Wolfgang. "Today, my son, your age demands you face your responsibilities.

You'll be a king soon, and you should have a wife. Tomorrow at the court ball you must choose your bride from among the beauties of the kingdom."

"Yes, mother. As you wish, of course." Siegfried, though displeased, responds with respect and kisses her hand.

The old queen departs, and the party becomes lively again. Anxious to forget the sudden burdens of adulthood, Siegfried dances long into the afternoon.

At sunset, the guests begin leaving. They toast the prince, say goodbye to Benno and Wolfgang, and return home. Siegfried stands alone, brooding over the future and what it holds.

Benno is sensitive to his friend's unhappy mood. "Come, Siegfried, let's spend the evening together. We'll return to the castle and . . . Wait! Do you hear that?"

A sweet, haunting melody fills the air, followed by the sound of flapping wings.

"Look! Wild swans. How beautiful they are! Why don't we take our bows and hunt them?" Benno suggests. But when he glances at Siegfried, he notices a changed expression on the prince's face. Siegfried appears enchanted, like a man under a spell. Without answering his friend, he picks up his crossbow and leaves in pursuit of the swans.

Act II

Moonlight illuminates a lake and a forest clearing blanketed by thick mist. Boulders and stone ruins emerge like islands from the white sea of vapor, and a strange form takes shape. An evil apparition—part bird, part man—rises and expands like a bat spreading its black wings. It is the sorcerer Von Rotbart, the cruelest of men. Jerking his head swiftly from side to side, he senses an intruder in his watery domain, and runs from the clearing to hide.

As the fog lifts, Siegfried approaches, drawn to this enchanted spot. He sees that the swans have settled on the lake and raises his bow, but something so strange happens that he is unable to shoot. The leading swan glides in his

*An evil apparition—part bird, part man—
rises and expands like a bat spreading its
black wings.*

direction, surrounded by a magic haze of light. As he watches in amazement, it changes form before his very eyes.

"What kind of swan is that? Is it a bird or a woman?" he wonders. The figure steps ashore timidly, and the curious prince hides in the tall grass to observe it more closely.

The creature has swan feathers adorning its hair, a dress of brilliant white plumage, and a golden crown upon its head. Though it moves with all the grace and gestures of a swan, it is a woman. Thinking she is alone, she stands motionless on one leg.

Siegfried advances quietly, cautiously, one soft step after another, but the swan-woman notices him and is frightened. Trembling, she backs away.

"Don't leave," he pleads. "I won't hurt you. You are the loveliest creature I've ever seen. I want only to protect you. Look, I'm putting down my bow."

His words seem to reassure her, and slowly she grows accustomed to his presence.

"Who are you? Where do you come from?" he asks.

"I am Odette, queen of the swans. That lake is made of my mother's tears. She filled it on the day that the wicked magician, Von Rotbart, took me away from her and imprisoned me in the shape of a swan. I'm only allowed to take human form between midnight and dawn."

Her story touches him. "How can I help you, Odette? I want to set you free, to make you smile and return you to the day."

"Only the true love of a man can save me. A man who will love no other, who will marry me and be loyal forever."

"I can be that man, Odette. From the moment I saw you, I've wanted to love and care for you,"

"It's not that simple. If I'm betrayed, I will never be allowed to become human again. I will be a swan always."

The black-cloaked figure of Von Rotbart enters the glade and destroys the calm of their meeting. Siegfried raises his bow to shoot, but the swan queen throws her body between them, fearing that if Von Rotbart is killed the spell will never be broken.

The sorcerer doesn't like to be threatened and hovers menacingly over the prince. Odette rushes to Siegfried's side and shelters her newfound love from this madman. Von Rotbart leaps to a high boulder, screams out his curses, and disappears into the night.

"You see, my prince, he'll stop at nothing to keep me with him."

"Odette, come to the ball in honor of my twenty-first birthday, and I'll choose you as my bride in front of the whole kingdom. Von Rotbart will then know that we are promised to each other, and he'll be forced to lift his spell."

"No, while he has this power over me, I am doomed to stay here. Only our marriage would free me to visit the castle as a real woman, not as a wild bird. But be careful, Siegfried, for he will try to trick you any way he can."

"Impossible! I am more determined than he. My love will overpower him."

Then Siegfried witnesses another astonishing sight. A wedge of beautiful swan maidens, dressed just like Odette, dances into the glade. The maidens fill the clearing, dancing with the symmetry of a flock of wild birds in flight, and form a corridor for their queen. Odette runs through the pathway, her arms fluttering, and at its end she embraces her waiting prince to the heavenly sound of violins. Siegfried follows her along a diagonal line of swans as she gently hops on one foot, her arms extended, her leg in arabesque. They dance a duet to passionate music, which at last gives way to tender strains, and Siegfried holds Odette's arms as if they were fragile wings, moving them toward her body and rocking her gently from side to side.

"I have enough love to free you," he says.

She leans on the prince, her body totally relaxed, and whispers, "Yes, I will place all my hopes on you."

A rhythmic melody begins, gay, yet tinged with sadness, and four swan maidens dance hand in hand, their heads tilting in the same direction, their melancholy expressions all the same. Dresses and feet bob up and down, moving quickly to the staccato sounds.

The sky grows lighter, and Odette arches like a swan about to fly. Assuming their positions in line, the maidens prepare to depart. They bounce on one foot to a marching rhythm which propels them toward the lake. It is the last dance of this magical night, and the melody that Siegfried heard when he first saw the swans returns.

"What is it, my love? Please don't go," he cries.

"I must. The sun is about to rise, and the others are leaving."

Von Rotbart emerges from the shadows. "Enough! Back to the water!" he screams, hypnotically drawing Odette to him.

The swan queen's arms reach out to Siegfried, but against her will her trembling legs carry her away. As the distance between them increases, Odette's arms obey Von Rotbart's magic and move once again in the undulating rhythms of a true swan.

Siegfried is left alone.

Swan Lake ACT II

Act III

The next evening, the queen's party for Prince Siegfried is under way in the castle's glittering ballroom. Tonight Siegfried must choose a wife, and his spirits are low. He thinks only of Odette.

Six of the loveliest maidens in the kingdom are announced and promenade before him. His mother's stern presence reminds him of his solemn duty.

"Greet them, son. Dance with them. They're waiting."

"Yes, mother. If you so wish."

He slowly spins each girl on his arm to a courtly waltz. His manner is distracted and he dances mechanically, for he has left his heart with Odette by the forest lake. When he finishes, flowers are brought to him by a servant.

"Siegfried," says the queen mother, "these flowers are to be given to the girl of your choice. They will signify your decision to marry and cherish only her."

Siegfried's chest heaves with despair, and his head bows. "No, it's impossible."

Before his worried mother can question him, trumpets announce the arrival of two strangers. The man is attired sumptuously in purple and black and claims to be a baron, but he looks suspiciously like the evil sorcerer. With him is his daughter, Odile, a ravishing beauty dressed in jet black. She looks enticingly familiar, and Siegfried is captivated by her. Her arms move in imitation of Odette's to an ominous melody, which echoes the swan queen's tragic theme. Unknown to Siegfried, the man is Von Rotbart, and he has transformed his own child into the image of Odette, in order to trick the prince. Just as the sorcerer had hoped, Siegfried abandons himself to this magical creature, believing that she is Odette.

"Your Highness, my daughter is of noble birth," says Von Rotbart with all the charm he can muster. "She would make an admirable match for your son, and indeed, they seem to be entranced with one another."

The queen reflects a moment and answers, "I have no objection to so lovely a girl, Baron."

Von Rotbart smirks with satisfaction and sits beside the queen. Together they greet the remaining guests—dignitaries and their attendants who have come from faraway lands to pay homage to the prince and perform their native dances.

When the display is finished, Von Rotbart requests that Odile be allowed to dance before the court. Signaling the musicians to play, he summons his daughter to take her place in the spotlight.

With a haughty look in her eye, Odile dances seductively, spinning in Siegfried's willing arms. She encourages him to join her, to dance close to her, but then she turns her head away and arrogantly denies him. While taking a long look at her father, Odile falls back into Siegfried's embrace. The prince is spellbound and completely in this mysterious beauty's power, until a cry in the distance disturbs his thoughts.

The swan queen has appeared in the castle window. She reaches out desperately for Siegfried, silently begging, "Please don't forget me." Von Rotbart too sees Odette, and commands his daughter to distract the prince. Again, Odile uses the swan queen's singular gesture, the beautiful waving arms that ripple like bird wings on water. Siegfried's mind clears. The arms have convinced him once more, and he dances happily, leaping higher and higher, prancing like a peacock, aglow with youth and desire.

Now Odile knows victory is near, and she displays her hold over the prince with a series of whipping turns. With each circle of her leg, she gathers speed and daring, until she finishes triumphantly.

"Mother, I'm sure. It's Odile I want to marry. Give me the flowers!"

But Von Rotbart is not satisfied. "Wait! First you must promise to love my daughter forever, to be true to her and her alone. Will you make that promise?"

"Yes, oh yes!" cries Siegfried. "I swear it. I will love only Odile."

The black swan accepts his bouquet.

Thunder crashes and it grows dark. Siegfried's doom is sealed.

"You young fool, it isn't Odile you want! There is your love." Von Rotbart points to Odette, the real swan queen, crying out her song of misery at the window.

Siegfried is horrified. "You've tricked me, just as Odette said you would."

Odile laughs at him and throws the bouquet at his feet in disgust. The flowers scatter everywhere. Then, in a blaze of fire, the evil sorcerer and his cruel daughter vanish.

"My dear Odette, what will become of us?" Siegfried sobs. He kisses his mother goodbye and runs off to the forest to find his true love.

Act IV

It is a dark and desperate night. The mist has an ominous glow to it and covers everything in sight. The swan maidens dance sadly through the glade, their steps gradually subduing the clouds of vapor. They wait anxiously for their queen.

Odette approaches her subjects. Her body, bent over with sobs, acknowledges the weight of her grief. She knows she has lost her one chance for love and life.

"I have come to say goodbye," she tells them. "Prince Siegfried has betrayed me, and Von Rotbart has won. I cannot imagine living forever as a swan, never to be human again, never to see Siegfried's face, or to know his love. I must die. It's the only way to free myself."

"No, you must wait for Siegfried. He has not willingly betrayed you. Someone so trusting could have no defense against the schemes of a sorcerer. He still loves you, Odette."

Bolts of lightning frighten the swan maidens into a flurry of movement, and thunderclaps sound in the distance. The maidens hover in small groups, comforting one another. Siegfried rushes in, searches among them, and at last discovers Odette, collapsed on the damp earth.

"Oh, my sweetest love, I thought I might never see you again, but Von Rotbart hasn't harmed you yet. Please don't weep, I never meant to hurt you. I was sure you were the baron's daughter. She looked like you, she moved like you. I wanted to declare my love for you in front of the whole kingdom and break the evil monster's spell. Tell me you understand."

"Oh, poor Siegfried! Yes, I understand and I do love you, but what does it matter now? Von Rotbart has destroyed our one chance for happiness with his fiendish tricks. You must see that my only escape is death—otherwise I will be imprisoned forever as one of his wild birds."

"No, there must be a way out. I will. . . ." But he is interrupted by the wicked sorcerer.

"I've won, Siegfried," laughs the magician. "Did you think you could save her? Never! I am master here. All of these creatures are in my power."

Von Rotbart lunges at the lovers, determined to separate them. The prince puts his hand up and prevents the villain from seizing Odette.

Swan Lake ACT III

"Farewell, my dearest," she whispers in Siegfried's ear. "Only in death can I love you."

Odette kisses him, runs to a high rock by the lake, and plunges to her death. Siegfried now knows what he must do. Following her steps, he mounts to the top of the same steep precipice and leaps.

Von Rotbart is stunned. All his schemes and vile plans have been ruined in the space of a heartbeat. A broken man, he falls to the ground, writhing in pain and defeat.

The sky glows pink in the dawning light and the maidens whisper, "Von Rotbart is dead." They bow in gratitude for their freedom, privileged to have seen a love as strong as Odette's and Siegfried's.

And on the water, shimmering in the morning sun, a boat glides by carrying the swan queen and her valiant prince to an eternity in the comfort of each other's arms.

— the curtain falls —

Siegfried at last discovers Odette, collapsed on the damp earth.

La Sylphide

Act I

From far, far away, a small, flickering light grows larger and brighter. Gradually it becomes a roaring fire and shines on the face of young James asleep in his chair. Shadows dance around him on the high ceiling and oak walls of an old farmhouse. But more than shadows dance here, for this is Scotland, where the misty air plays tricks on willing dreamers. It comes as no surprise to see a delicate fairy, dressed in white, appear from these foggy surroundings. She gazes at the sleeping man, her eyes full of love. Will she be gone like a dream when he awakes?

"Are you real?" he murmurs, and tries to catch her to find out. She steps aside nervously, arms quivering, head darting. He grabs only fistfuls of air.

"My handsome young man was so peaceful and still. Why is he chasing me now? I must fly away!" Her fluttering wings carry her to the fireplace and she disappears up the chimney.

The bewildered young dreamer searches every inch of the room. All he finds is his best friend, Gurn, dozing in a corner.

"Did you see what I just saw?" James cries.

"What are you talking about, James? See what? I've been napping."

"You won't believe this, but I've just seen a beautiful fairy sprite."

"Where is she?" asks Gurn.

"Vanished . . . she simply dissolved into thin air. I think I scared her away."

"James, this is nonsense. You shouldn't be dreaming of someone else, today of all days. You're getting married in a few hours to a splendid girl, so don't go thinking of other loves. It isn't right."

La Sylphide ACT I

La Sylphide ACT II

Gurn ends his advice angrily, head wagging, feet stamping. He too loves James's bride-to-be, and his jealousy is showing.

"Calm down, Gurn. Effie is coming. I promise I'll forget my sprite."

But James continues to daydream, and Gurn is the first to welcome the bride. Effie notices the change in her groom right away.

"What's the matter, James?" she asks. "Aren't you going to kiss me?"

He blushes, embarrassed that his heart is so far away, and kisses her lovingly. They are interrupted by festive music as Effie's bridesmaids burst into the room and encircle her with warm wishes. James steps back to admire his bride.

"Yes," he thinks, "I'm a lucky man to be marrying such a wonderful girl."

But his attention quickly wanders over to a dark corner near the fireplace, where he last saw the fairy. Someone is moving in the shadows, and James rushes to the spot.

"I knew she would come back to me," he whispers.

But he is mistaken and jumps back in terror. Out of the shadows stalks Old Madge, a hideous witch with long, stringy, gray hair and ragged clothes. She is the village sorceress, and the laughter from James's house has drawn her out of the forest. Everyone seems willing to have her join the festivities, but James's disappointment has made him furious.

"This is my wedding day! What do you think you're doing here without an invitation? Get out!"

Effie and her bridesmaids are surprised that James could be so unkind, and beg Madge to stay and tell their fortunes.

"What do you see in my palm, Old Madge? Does James love me?" the bride teases.

Old Madge cackles, determined to upset James. "Your charming bridegroom doesn't love you best, young lady. There's one who loves you more."

"That's enough," James cries. "Get out, you ugly witch. Out! Out!"

Madge nods her head and, with a knowing glint in her eye, allows herself to be pushed out through the door.

"James, you really must love me to risk tangling with Old Madge." And, indeed, at this moment James does seem to be in love with Effie.

"Now I must hurry upstairs and put on my wedding veil," Effie says, and kisses her groom goodbye.

James, alone in his living room, paces the floor. He can't get the sprite off his mind. His thoughts of her are so vivid that they seem to inhabit the very air. He feels cold . . . he feels hot. The wind rushes by, and suddenly a light drives open the window. The light moves forward and frames his fairy sprite, who never touches the ground, but hovers at the window's edge.

In a comforting, gentle voice, she speaks.

"I am the Sylphide, my home is the sky and the trees. If you get married today, I'll surely die. You see, I love you."

She dances before him, a dance of sadness and longing. Never before has he seen legs move so delicately, arms so gracefully, or hands so tenderly. He tries to resist her, but it's hopeless. Her silent tears compel him to confess his love for her. Knowing her love is returned, she dances joyfully, and James is enraptured. Forgetting his promise to love Effie, he kisses the Sylphide.

"Aha!" thinks Gurn, who is hiding in the shadows. "Now Effie must be told the truth." He hurries up the stairs.

Poor Effie, wearing her wedding veil and followed by the bridal guests, rushes in upon hearing Gurn's news. Frightened, the Sylphide hides in a chair, beneath a tartan cape.

"Watch this, everyone. Here is James's secret," cries Gurn. He pulls the cape away in triumph.

"But no one is there," shouts the crowd.

The Sylphide is no ordinary being with earthbound feet, and she has vanished again.

Gurn is astounded, the bride feels foolish, and the guests assume that jealousy has made Gurn lose his reason. Effie turns to James and begs, "Please, let's begin the wedding celebration before anything else happens."

The bagpipes announce a Scottish reel, and the guests dance joyously. To the lively music, James spins Effie on his arm. Round and round they dance until, invisible to everyone but James, the Sylphide returns. She takes his other arm and is dancing too. Every step that Effie takes is copied by the Sylphide, only higher in the air, and in a frantic struggle to make both girls happy, James is partnering not one but two loves. His strange behavior puzzles the guests, but the ceremony is about to begin and no one has a chance to ask him what is wrong.

James looks into Effie's eyes. "Here is the wedding ring," he says, reaching for her finger.

What ring? It is gone, snatched away by the unhappy Sylphide. She flies to the door, beckoning James to follow. He hesitates only a minute and then runs after her, leaving behind his home, his friends, and a sad, sad bride.

Act II

In a deep, black forest, ugly witches gather round a steaming pot concocting something horrible. Old Madge fishes in the brew and pulls out a long silk scarf. She runs away cackling, very happy with herself and the mischief she is making.

*   *   *

The forest walls lighten with the day, and James appears, looking left and right and up and down, searching for his Sylphide. The fairy sprite plucks a bird's nest from a nearby tree and flies down beside James to show him her treasure. Overjoyed to find his love, James reaches out for her but is suddenly surrounded by a group of delicate sylphs. As they dance, the Sylphide flutters among them, then disappears. James is beginning to wonder if he made a mistake leaving home for this illusive sprite. She never stays still for long. Every time he tries to talk to her or hold her, she flies into the air, darting from tree to cloud. In his house, she had to disappear to avoid being caught, but here in the forest there is no reason for her to vanish.

Alone in the forest, James is feeling very sorry for himself when he happens upon Madge. But this time, instead of being angry with her, he's glad to see a familiar face.

"Madge, can you forgive me for my rudeness yesterday? I don't know what came over me."

"I understand," Madge says in her high, scratchy voice. "Don't worry about it. You look so gloomy, young man. What's the trouble?"

He's very glad to have someone to confide in. "I'm so unhappy. The sylph I gave up everything for isn't behaving at all as I expected."

"And what did you expect?"

In a deep, black forest, ugly witches gather round a steaming pot concocting something horrible.

"I expected her to be like any normal girl, to walk hand in hand in the forest and spend long evenings with me, but she's always flying away—disappearing into the air with other winged sprites just like her."

"I have just the thing for you," Madge says slyly. "Here's a charmed cloth that will solve all your problems."

123

She presents James with the silk scarf and tells him what to do.

"If you wrap this around your Sylphide, she won't go anywhere. She'll stay with you forever, right here on earth where you think you want her, instead of in the clouds."

James thanks Madge over and over again, and then goes off to find the Sylphide. He discovers her in the trees and holds up the magic scarf. Like earthly mortals, she loves presents, and she flies down beside him.

"What is it, James? Is it for me? Oh please, may I put it on? Will you put it round me?"

James teases her a little. Playfully, he flings one end of the scarf into the air, then pulls it back again before she can grab hold.

"Come, James, give me the scarf," she begs.

"All right, my love. Come here."

He drapes the scarf over the Sylphide's shoulders and winds it twice around her arms. The forest is silent, the music stops. As the cloth touches her, she grows weak. Her wings tremble and break away. She is no longer able to stand, and James must support her—but it's no use. To a tragic melody, she slips through his arms and sinks to the ground. James doesn't know what is happening, and the Sylphide can't understand why he has done this awful thing to her. When Madge's cackle echoes in the forest, James realizes the terrible truth.

"She's dying," he cries, "and it's my fault! What is life worth without her?"

As James looks on, the dead Sylphide is lifted into the sky, cradled in the arms of her sisters. Faraway bells break the silence. James gazes into the distance and sees a bride and groom march past hand in hand. The bells James hears are wedding bells, ringing for Effie and Gurn and the bright future that awaits them.

The sad young man realizes he has lost two loves today. Perhaps if James finds love again, he'll know better how to keep it.

— the curtain falls —

Illustrator's Note

The paintings are done on 140 lb. D'Arches Aquarelle hot press paper. I use Winsor and Newton tube watercolors. The black-and-white illustrations are done in lamp black, a much richer and subtler black than ivory. I paint with Kolinsky sable brushes, because they hold the most satisfactory points. I use a 000 brush for the most delicate lines and details, using pen and ink only for straight edges and architectural details.

For the color illustrations, I first do a series of pencil sketches. I then do a rough drawing the size of the final art—$12\frac{3}{8}''\times 10\frac{9}{16}''$. This is redrawn and transferred to watercolor paper. I generally use a lightly tinted watercolor wash as an underpainting, adding broad areas of color next. I paint my details last.

A good deal of the inspiration for these paintings can be found in the many notable ballet productions themselves, whose set and costume designers, in my mind, contribute as much to the drama and charm of the great story ballets as do the choreographers, composers, and dancers.

Some Information on the Ballets

The following list gives the background to the ballets on which the stories in this book are based. When these are not the earliest productions, the first performances of the original versions are also mentioned.

Cinderella

Music by Sergei Prokofiev. Choreography by Frederick Ashton. Based on the fairy tale by Charles Perrault. First presented by the Sadler's Wells Ballet at Covent Garden, London, on December 23, 1948. Earliest version choreographed by Rotislav Zakharov; first presented by the Bolshoi Ballet at the Bolshoi Theater, Moscow, on November 15, 1945.

Coppélia

Music by Léo Delibes. Choreography by Arthur Saint-Léon. Book by Saint-Léon and Charles Nuitter based on *The Sandman* by E.T.A. Hoffmann. First presented at the Opéra, Paris, on May 25, 1870.

Don Quixote

Music by Ludwig Minkus. Choreography by Marius Petipa. Based on the novel by Cervantes. First presented at the Bolshoi Theater, Moscow, on December 26, 1869.

La Fille Mal Gardée

Music by Ferdinand Hérold. Choreography by Frederick Ashton. First presented by the Royal Ballet at Covent Garden, London, on January 28, 1960. Earliest version choreographed by Jean Dauberval; first presented at the Grand Théâtre, Bordeaux, on July 1, 1789.

Firebird

Music by Igor Stravinsky. Choreography by Michel Fokine. Based on a number of Russian folk tales by A. Afanasiev. First presented by Diaghilev's Ballets Russes at the Opéra, Paris, on June 25, 1910.

Giselle

Music by Adolpe Adam. Choreography by Jules Perrot and Jean Coralli. Book by Vernoy de Saint-Georges, Théophile Gautier, and Jean Coralli. First presented at the Opéra, Paris, on June 28, 1841.

Some Information on the Ballets

The Nutcracker

Music by Peter Ilyich Tchaikovsky. Choreography by George Balanchine. Based on *The Nutcracker and the King of Mice* by E.T.A. Hoffmann. First presented by the New York City Ballet at City Center, New York, on February 2, 1954. Earliest version choreographed by Lev Ivanov; first presented at the Maryinsky Theater, St. Petersburg, on December 18, 1892.

Petrouchka

Music by Igor Stravinsky. Choreography by Michel Fokine. Scenery and costumes by Alexandre Benois. Book by Stravinsky and Benois. First presented by Diaghilev's Ballets Russes at the Théâtre du Châtelet, Paris, on June 13, 1911.

Romeo and Juliet

Music by Sergei Prokofiev. Choreography by Kenneth MacMillan. Based on the play by William Shakespeare. First presented by the Royal Ballet at Covent Garden, London, on February 9, 1965. Earliest version choreographed by Leonid Lavrovsky; first presented at the Kirov State Theater, Leningrad, on January 11, 1940.

The Sleeping Beauty

Music by Peter Ilyich Tchaikovsky. Choreography by Marius Petipa. Additional dances by Kenneth MacMillan. Based on the fairy tale by Charles Perrault. First presented by the Royal Ballet at Covent Garden, London, on March 15, 1973. Earliest version first presented at the Maryinsky Theater, St. Petersburg, on January 15, 1890.

Swan Lake

Music by Peter Ilyich Tchaikovsky. Choreography by Lev Ivanov and Marius Petipa. Book by V.P. Begitchev and Vasily Geltzer. First presented at the Maryinsky Theater, St. Petersburg, on January 27, 1895. Earliest version choreographed by Jules Reisinger; first presented at the Bolshoi Theater, Moscow, on March 4, 1877.

La Sylphide

The author's story is based on the following two versions:
Music by Jean Schneitzhoeffer. Choreography by Filippo Taglioni. Book by Adolphe Nourrit. First presented at the Opéra, Paris, on March 12, 1832.
Music by Herman Løvenskjold. Choreography by Auguste Bournonville. Book by Adolphe Nourrit. First presented by the Royal Danish Ballet at the Royal Theater, Copenhagen, on November 28, 1836.

Acknowledgments

My very special gratitude is due Robert Porter whose support, encouragement, and invaluable criticism were always forthcoming. For their research assistance, my thanks to Wini Messe and the staff of the Dance Collection, The New York Public Library, Lincoln Center; and for his help in gathering many videotapes of the productions, my appreciation to David Jacobs. I am also deeply grateful to Merrill Ashley for her insights and help and to Kibbe Fitzpatrick for his interest in this project.